This story is dedicated to the men of the United States 9ᵗʰ Army who liberated my comrades and me on April 12, 1945, and to the International Red Cross, which kept us alive.

Destined to Survive

A Dieppe Veteran's Story

Jack A. Poolton
and Jayne Poolton-Turvey

To Harold   *June 2000*

Jack A Poolton

DUNDURN PRESS
TORONTO · OXFORD

Editor: Barry Jowett
Design: Scott Reid
Printer: Transcontinental Printing Inc.

Canadian Cataloguing in Publication Data
Destined to survive
Poolton, Jack A., 1918-

ISBN 1-55002-311-X
1. Poolton, Jack A., 1918- . 2. World War, 1939-1945 — Personal narratives, Canadian. 3. Dieppe Raid, 1942 — Personal narratives.
I. Poolton-Turvey, Jayne, 1958- . II. Title

D811.P66 1998   940.54'21425   C98-931580-0

2   3   4   5   02   01   00   99

THE CANADA COUNCIL | LE CONSEIL DES ARTS
FOR THE ARTS | DU CANADA
SINCE 1957 | DEPUIS 1957

We acknowledge the support of the Canada Council for the Arts for our publishing program. We also acknowledge the support of the Ontario Arts Council and the Book Publishing Industry Development Program of the Department of Canadian Heritage.

Care has been taken to trace the ownership of copyright material used in this book. The author and the publisher welcome any information enabling them to rectify any references or credit in subsequent editions.

Printed and bound in Canada.

Printed on recycled paper.

Dundurn Press
8 Market Street
Suite 200
Toronto, Ontario, Canada
M5E 1M6

Dundurn Press
73 Lime Walk
Headington, Oxford,
England
OX3 7AD

Dundurn Press
2250 Military Road
Tonawanda NY
U.S.A 14150

Contents

 Jack A. Poolton was a private in "D" Company of the Royal Regiment, Canadian Second Division, in World War II. After the war he worked as a mechanic until retirement at age 65. He and his wife, Colette, have three children and nine grandchildren.

Preface

by Jayne Poolton-Turvey

It was fifty years before my father was able to put his story into words. After having gone through all the traumatic events during his time overseas, he discovered that settling down and fitting back into regular society was somewhat of a challenge. He knew during his time as a POW that when and if he returned home, the occupation he chose would have to be something that would hold his interest and not be boring.

Certain people in his life thought they knew better than he what direction his life should take. This added to the stress he was experiencing. He tried his hand at several things that did not work out, including applying to rejoin the army. Veteran's Affairs was offering a mechanics course, and he decided that was

Jack's dog tag.

what he would do. Apparently this was a good decision as the work never seemed to be boring, and he was working on something different each day.

However, he suffered from a duodenal ulcer, constant headaches, and bouts of depression. He realized he was living with a terrible handicap. Not known until recently, when a study was done on Dieppe POWs and their return home, most ex-prisoners of war were suffering from post-traumatic stress disorder, a serious mental illness that none of these men were ever treated for. This would include nightmares, flashbacks, and various other stress symptoms. However, in spite of all these drawbacks, as well as surviving a fractured neck in 1971 in a terrible car accident, he worked as a mechanic until his retirement at 65.

Jack married Colette Desrosiers after the war and raised three children, Janet, Jack Jr., and Jayne, and has nine grandchildren.

Jack's Combined Operation insignia.

Foreword

Destined to Survive is a factual book written not by a journalist, war correspondent, or ghost writer, but by a private soldier who lived the experience for almost three years, lived with the memory for the next fifty-three years, and has now told his story. Jack Poolton was captured during the ill-fated Dieppe raid and spent the rest of the war as a prisoner of the Germans in a number of camps under the most deplorable conditions. This is not a fanciful tale, but rather an account of the day-to-day experiences of a brave young soldier as he remembers them now. I believe you will enjoy this true saga and perhaps, as I did, feel the pain, the bitterness, the anxiety, the hope, and the exhilaration this man felt while in his early twenties. His story exemplifies the human spirit and demonstrates the determination one needs to survive the appalling circumstances. One must salute this soldier, and all others who sacrificed so much to preserve the freedom we take for granted. This book should be required reading in our classrooms.

William C. Stark, CD, LCol (ret'd)
48th Highlanders of Canada
23 September 1998

One
Joining Up

It was 1939. Due to the Depression, employment was extremely scarce. Twenty-one-year-old Jack Poolton, a native of Kapuskasing, Ontario, had travelled to Watson, Saskatchewan, where he had found work on a farm harvesting wheat. After working there for a few months, rumours of war had penetrated this small prairie town. And finally, on September 3, 1939, official reports marked the beginning of the Second World War. Jack had always wanted to be a soldier, and finally the chance had come.

When war broke out, I had conflicting thoughts. My father, who had been in the Great War, had told us terrible stories that gave us nightmares as children. But thoughts of adventure kept entering my mind, and I felt a tremendous amount of loyalty to my King and country. Also, there were few jobs available as a result of the Depression.

My decision to join up was confirmed the night I heard radio reports of the sinking of the British passenger ship *Athenia* by a German submarine. As there were few radios in the area, and we were anxious to hear any news of the war, I happened to be sitting in a German home listening to the radio. The German woman was smiling and ringing her hands with glee as she heard the report. I was shocked to see her reaction and decided that the submarine service had to be the most cowardly. And now with Canada at war, I had to join up as soon as possible.

I travelled to Saskatoon with the intention of joining the army.

At the armouries, men were lined up waiting to enlist. Word was the locals would be given priority. As I was from Ontario, I decided to return home, but on the way I stopped in Winnipeg to try and sign up there. As I stood outside the Winnipeg Union Station, I was amazed by the first parade and the first pipe band I had ever seen. It was the Queen's Own Cameron Highlanders. Little did I know at the time that two years later I would get to know a lot of these men as POWs in Germany.

I was unable to enlist there either, so I returned home to Kapuskasing to spend the winter working for my father at his Ford Dealership.

I was eager to leave home and become a soldier, so in April 1940, I took the last money I had in the bank to buy a train ticket for Toronto, hoping that I would be able to join up there.

After a twelve hour train ride, I arrived in Toronto and went directly to the Canadian National Exhibition Grounds. There was a hustle and bustle of activity. Soldiers were parading up and down the streets, and young men were lining up eagerly waiting to become soldiers. The Royal Regiment of Canada was taking recruits inside the Government Building. That was where I headed.

My father had advised me to stay away from the infantry, as he had served in the infantry in the Great War. But all I wanted to do was join up, whether it was infantry or not, and as I had poor eyesight, we discussed over and over again what I should do. The conclusion was that I should memorize at least three of the smaller lines of the eye chart during my medical examination. At the University Avenue armouries, I passed everything with flying colours … except my eye test. Although I had tried to memorize the eye chart, I ended up reading off the wrong letters.

A higher ranking officer was called in. He asked me, "Do you really want to join the army?"

My reply was, "Yes, sir."

I explained that I had just paid my way from Kapuskasing to Toronto for the purpose of joining up. The officer said, "You are now a soldier in the Royal Regiment of Canada."

Here I was, in an infantry regiment … after I'd been warned! April 20, 1940: the day I became a "Royal." I felt like a somebody that day.

After I had taken the oath, and sworn to serve anywhere, it was time to start soldiering and earn my $1.30 a day. Most of the

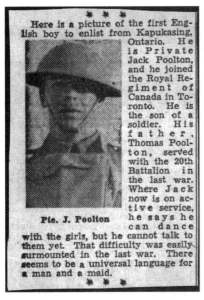

Here is a picture of the first English boy to enlist from Kapuskasing, Ontario. He is Private Jack Poolton, and he joined the Royal Regiment of Canada in Toronto. He is the son of a soldier. His father, Thomas Poolton, served with the 20th Battalion in the last war. Where Jack now is on active service, he says he can dance with the girls, but he cannot talk to them yet. That difficulty was easily surmounted in the last war. There seems to be a universal language for a man and a maid.

Pte. J. Poolton

Newspaper clipping that appeared in the Kapuskasing Northern Times shortly after Jack enlisted.

training would take place on the Canadian National Exhibition Grounds in Toronto. During the first week I was issued a uniform, rifle, bayonet, and equipment. We were given instructions on handling the rifle safely. Then the rifle and squad drill started, along with bayonet practice, route marches, and guard duty. I was starting to feel like a soldier.

After about a month, they told me that if I had any business at home that needed to be taken care of, I could apply for a forty-eight hour leave. They would supply me with a train ticket to Kapuskasing.

It was a great feeling being back in my hometown in uniform. My parents did not believe that I would be going overseas right away, but I knew deep down that it would be a long time before I would see them again. After putting my affairs in order, it was time to leave. At the station, I slowly climbed the steps of the train and gazed sadly at the familiar faces around me. As the train began to move, I waved goodbye until my family became a speck on the station platform. With a tear in my eye and an ache in my heart I left my hometown of Kapuskasing where I had spent such a happy childhood. I could see my family's farm from the train and as we picked up speed, the farm became lost in the distance. I had to look away.

This turned out to be my first and only leave in Canada before leaving the country.

Early in May 1940, the "Royals" boarded trains bound for Camp Borden where we completed our basic training. While at Camp Borden, we were issued winter underwear, cardigans, and greatcoats. (Apparently we were being equipped for a cold climate.) On June 8, 1940, we boarded trains once again, under cover of darkness, this time bound for Halifax, Nova Scotia, where we embarked on the S.S. *Empress of Australia*. I was amazed at the size of this great ship, which was to take us safely across the dangerous Atlantic. This ship had carried King George VI and Queen Elizabeth across the Atlantic in 1939, just a few months before the war broke out.

At around 13:00 hours on June 11, the S.S. *Empress of Australia* began creeping out of Halifax Harbour, accompanied by the British Cruiser H.M.S. *Emerald* and a destroyer. At 18:00 hours the destroyer turned around and headed back. The two ships proceeded to cross the Atlantic. We were then told that they were not headed for the United Kingdom, but for Iceland, land of the midnight sun.

S.S. *Empress of Australia*.

H.M.S. *Emerald*.

Two

The Land of the Midnight Sun

By the spring of 1940, the Germans had taken Norway and the British expected that their next move would be Iceland. This would be disastrous for Allied ships crossing the ocean, as the Germans would be in command of the North Atlantic. The Royal Regiment was the most available regiment, and so they were chosen to bolster the British forces that were already there. They would be part of "Z" Force and wear the polar bear on their sleeve.

We arrived at Reykjavik, Iceland, at midnight on June 16, 1940, with the sun still shining. We were immediately unloaded off the ship, as a German submarine had been reported in the area. Before leaving the ship, we were told that the majority of the people were hostile and that it was possible that some of them might spit in our faces. If this happened, we were told not to retaliate, as we were visitors, not invaders.

The British were there with transport to take us to a camp where tents had already been set up for us. It rained for the next eight or nine days, which was very depressing.

One night early in our stay in Iceland, I was assigned the duty of guarding a huge ordinance dump that was in an unused fish factory on the outskirts of Reykjavik. At about 02:00 hours, while I was standing guard with my buddy, Private Pettigrew, I observed a light coming from a fourth floor window along the front street of Reykjavik. The light was flashing a type of code that was being answered by a ship out at sea. After watching this

15

light for several minutes, I came to the conclusion that this should be reported. As the platoon was stationed at least a kilometre away, I left Pettigrew, which was against orders, to double back to the platoon to report what I had seen. After being challenged by the guard, I was allowed to wake up the sergeant, who ordered two men to get dressed immediately and follow him. I left them and doubled back to my post, where Pettigrew was still observing the light.

It was later rumoured that German agents had been picked up in that building, signalling a produce ship from Argentina. They were telling the ship to leave the area, as a British cruiser was in the harbour. I believe this ship was later commandeered by the British cruiser and brought into port. Even though I had left my post, which was against all rules, I never heard the end result, and I was never questioned as to why I had left Pettigrew.

Shortly after this episode, D Company was moved to Hafnarfjordur, where we were stationed in an unused fish factory. After two months, we were suddenly moved to a place called Alafoss due to a skirmish between soldiers and some civilians. The confrontation was a result of the soldiers taking a dim view of Icelandic girls having their beautiful blonde hair shaved off in public because they had been seen with Canadian or British soldiers.

Before leaving Hafnarfjordur, we had to form a line and pick up everything visible to the eye. This included cigarette butts, matches, and gum wrappers. The building and area had to be left spotless. This was the standard procedure whenever the regiment moved.

During our stay we observed a number of cultural differences between Iceland and Canada. For example, it was the norm in Iceland that both sexes used the same toilets. It was also common for men and women to swim nude together. (Of course, all this was out of bounds to military personnel.) Crime, meanwhile, was almost non-existent. In years gone by, Icelandic punishment for serious crimes was death by drowning.

While in Iceland, soldiers had to go around in pairs, as it was dangerous to go anywhere alone. If you went on leave into Reykjavik, a pass was made out for two men. We always had to carry rifle, ammunition, steel helmet, and gas mask everywhere we went.

While at Alafoss, we dug a tank trap across a valley between two mountain ranges. It was apparent that this was the only place the Germans could land tanks by aircraft. The digging was done by hand, pick, and shovel, which turned into a tremendous undertaking. As well, "D" Company was involved in building defences and constructing a road, which later led to the airport. We also manned gun positions at crossroads, stopping and checking Icelandic vehicles. The Icelandic roads were so narrow that the rails had to be knocked off the bridges to get our trucks across.

One Sunday morning, there was an alert that a German invasion fleet was heading toward Iceland from Norway. Extra ammunition was passed around, and there was a general stand-to. However, nothing developed. Around this time, I was transferred to 16 Platoon. Prior to this, I had been in a reserve company.

While on a sightseeing tour, in a thirty-hundred-weight truck, the right front wheel came off and the truck overturned, spilling all its occupants out onto the lava rock that covers much of the island. Luckily, I was not one of the injured.

This land was very strange. We could stand in the middle of a stream and wash and shave, because the water on one side of the stream was hot and the other side was cold. There were several hot springs here; one had been tapped and was continually pouring boiling water out of a ten-inch pipe. It was later piped to heat the city of Reykjavik. One of our chaps accidentally slipped into the overflow and was badly scalded.

While at Alafoss we held a Regimental Sports Day. The Royal Marines challenged the Canadians to a game of soccer, and so I got to play soccer for the first time. It was great fun, butt I never got to kick the ball once.

I always felt sad when I saw ships leaving Iceland's shores. It made me feel homesick.

Prior to the Royals leaving Iceland for Scotland, we were taken out into a secluded valley and notified by the colonel that we would be leaving for England to join the Second Division. This was the best news I'd heard in six months. A few days later I was sitting with other Royals in a restaurant in Reykjavik. Lord Haw Haw (William Joyce, the traitor) made a radio announcement from Germany in English stating that the Royal Regiment was leaving for England shortly and that their ship would be sunk on the way there. As there had been no one close enough to hear what was said that day, other than members of the Regiment, I wondered how and where he could have received this information. (Despite the threat, we reached Scotland safely.)

The *Empress of Australia* sailed on the morning of October 31 with the Royal Regiment on board. Also sailing at that time were the H.M.T. *Antonia*, carrying the Second Division troops of the FMR (Les Fusiliers Mont-Royal), and the auxiliary cruiser *Latitia*. The Ottawa Cameron Highlanders, a machine-gun regiment and part of the Third Division, were left behind to spend the winter in Iceland. As we bade farewell to this odd country, we were piped off by the Camerons' pipe band playing "Will ye no come back again." I felt sorry that the Camerons were being left behind.

We left Iceland one day short of qualifying for the North Atlantic Star — a medal awarded for service in the North Atlantic. Also, the rum ration and fifty cigarettes a week we had been receiving while a part of British "Z" Force would now be discontinued.

Sailing at the worst time of the year, the North Sea was very rough, and the waters were very dangerous. Almost everyone was sea sick on the way over, except myself. It seemed like I was the only person that was in the mess hall to eat. (Maybe I should have joined the Navy.)

We finally arrived and sailed up the Clyde River to Gourock. After disembarking the *Empress of Australia*, we boarded trains for Aldershot. I was excited to finally reach the United Kingdom and I could hardly believe how beautiful and peaceful Scotland looked compared to the desolate landscape of Iceland.

Three
Joining the Second Division

At Gourock, the Royals boarded a train headed for Aldershot. Their first stop was the city of Carlisle, where English women had tea and sandwiches waiting on the station platform. It made the men feel good to hear the women with their beautiful English accents, and all along the railway, people were waving white sheets and pillow cases from their windows. It was a pleasure for the men to be able to speak to the people, who were quite a contrast from the people of Iceland.

Jack in England, 1940.

19

Travelling all night, we finally arrived at Aldershot, where we were met by pipe bands from the Canadian Second Division (Black Watch and Essex Scottish), who piped us to our barracks. It really felt great to be in England, where we had beds, running water, mess halls, and parade grounds. The best parts were the English pubs, canteens, and, of course, the women.

While at Aldershot, during the day we brushed up on our training, as we had done very little in Iceland. At night we would go to sleep listening to the bombing of London some forty miles away. At all times it was mandatory that all ranks carry steel helmets and gas masks — even when going to the latrine.

When it came time for me to take my first leave, I decided that I would like to journey to Birmingham, as that was where my father had been born. After I got off the train, I went into Grey's Department Store, where there was a real nice restaurant with an orchestra playing seasonal Christmas music. As I stood at the entrance, the head waitress came over to me with a message that I would honour a lady by sitting at her table and having dinner with her. I accepted the lady's invitation, and we shared a full-course turkey dinner. Before she got up to leave, my companion paid for my dinner. As her son was serving in the Middle East, she invited me to her home for Christmas. I thanked her, but I was unable to accept her invitation as I had aunts and uncles that were expecting me to spend Christmas

Jack in Birmingham, England, 1940.

with them. (I had a number of relatives in England at the time: two aunts — both my Dad's sisters — and several uncles and cousins. I visited them a number of times while in England.)

After returning from Christmas leave in Birmingham, the regiment was moved to Brighton. This was the regiment's first duty at coastal defence. My platoon, number 16, had an outpost high up on the downs and was also responsible for guarding the gas pumps on the Brighton road.

"D" Company was stationed in Lewes. I was in Lewes for New Years, 1941, and went to a New Year's Dance, where I met and danced with a very nice young lady. I recall she was wearing a Royal Stewart tartan skirt that night. I foolishly introduced her to my friend Jack Stewart only to discover later that he was dating her while I was on guard duty.

Fortunately, I met another girl, Daphne Rawlins. (Her father, being a church minister, had probably warned her to stay away from Canadian Soldiers. When walking her home I would have to leave her at least a block away from her house.) By coincidence, my brother Allan met Daphne at the church canteen three years later, and she still remembered me.

The women in England were very leery of married men. If a man wore a ring on his left hand the women would think the man was married. Some men would remove their rings, but there would still be the tell-tale mark. As I was wearing the ring my dad had worn in World War I, I was often suspected of being married, even though I was single.

My stay in Lewes left me with a lot of pleasant memories. We were always treated royally by the British people. It was a privilege to share the hardships and perils of war with them. The English kids would come to our camps to get the comics out of the *Star Weekly* and ask for gum. (There was a saying: "Got any gum chum?") To my knowledge, not one child was ever harmed by a Canadian soldier; they were completely safe.

During our stay in England, Canadians were often invited to go out and work on farms. Although I had put my name in several times, and was looking forward to farm work, I was never lucky enough to have the opportunity, even though I was the only man in "D" Company who had been raised on a farm, knew how to milk a cow, and could drive a team of horses.

Early in 1941, my brother Allan, who had also joined the army, wrote to me asking that I claim him into the regiment, as he was desperate to get overseas. I approached Captain Carter, second in command of "D" Company, who advised me to give it serious thought, as Allan was in the armoured corps with the rank of sergeant, earning trades pay at that time. Captain Carter also reminded me that the Royals were a foot-slogging outfit and I may not be doing my brother a favour bringing him into the regiment. If I decided to claim him, he would arrange to have my brother with the regiment within a fortnight. I gave it very serious thought before deciding not to follow it up. The fact that one of nearly every set of brothers in the regiment was killed at Dieppe proved that I had made the right decision.

On hearing that Pete Kelly and Frank Sheldon from my hometown were in England at Witley Camp, I decided that, when I got my next weekend pass, I would go and visit them. During that leave, strangers were giving me their names and numbers, hoping I could help get them into the regiment, as they were desperate to get away from the holding unit. Early on Monday, I approached Captain Carter once again and handed him a list of ten names and asked if he could get them sent to the regiment — and "D" Company — if possible. He asked me if they were all good soldiers. I assured him that they were. He said he would see what he could do.

We left that week on a manoeuvre, and I thought no more about it.

On returning to the barracks, I was amazed to find Pete Kelly, who was there with Red Perry and Jim Mawbey. Pete, of course, I had known from home; I was meeting Red and Jim for the first time. I soon found out that, in addition to these men — who became good friends of mine — all ten men whose names I had given to Captain Carter were now in "D" Company, and five of them were in my platoon. All these men fit well into the company. Frank Sheldon, meanwhile, had been sent to London and was on fire-watch duty at Canadian Military Headquarters. He had volunteered for fire-watch duty the day before the draft was sent to the regiment, and so he was unavailable for the draft. (I managed to see Frank several times when in London.)

While we were still at Aldershot, I took my drivers' test on trucks and passed. I had been told to forget the way I had learned to drive in Canada: now, I would be driving the army way. (The hardest part was driving on the opposite side of the road and having to change gears with the left hand.)

Our next move took us to Winchelsea Beach. This was the location where William the Conqueror chose to land in 1066. (He also made another landing at Pevonsley Bay near Hastings.) The Normans who landed on Winchelsea Beach were let up into the town of Winchelsea by a traitor who had raised the portcullis at what is still known as Traitor's Gate. Recalling William's successful invasions, the British intelligence figured that the Germans might choose to land in the same locations. There were rumours that the Germans had landed men at Winchelsea Beach in order to scout the location for a possible invasion. We were sometimes sent to patrol the beach, looking for German footprints. We never found any.

We were in a fortified house on the Channel Coast. All the cottages along the beach had been bulldozed, so that Germans could not take cover behind them. There were many dummy gun positions and blockhouses along the beach. There would be a circle of sand bags with a camouflaged light pole or telephone pole sticking out. From the air this would look like a heavy gun position. (The "blockhouses," I discovered, were made of plywood and cardboard camouflaged to look like the real thing. This was quite a contrast from what we were to face later, on the opposite side of the channel, where they were all made of reinforced concrete.)

While at Winchelsea Beach, several incidents happened. I was on guard with George Jones one night when we heard a strange noise, which sounded like someone walking on broken glass. Receiving no reply from a challenge, Jones fired his rifle. This brought the whole platoon out to find out what was wrong. We never did find out what the noise was.

On another occasion, as we were changing guards, which we did every two hours, one of the men accidentally placed a case of Bren gun magazines on a button that was used in the blockhouse to signal the platoon. This meant the signal would continually ring, causing a panic.

Still another time, while visiting Hastings with another soldier, we went to the arcade, where he met a young lady. Then we both went our separate ways. Later, when we met, he told me that she was Italian. As a senior soldier, I said "be careful what you say to her," seeing as we were at war with Italy. He met her later on and told her what I had said. She came at me like a lioness, claiming that I had said that she was an Italian sympathizer and should not be trusted. I could not believe that he had done this, and on returning to the platoon, I reported this to the officer. He told me that I had done the right thing and that soldiers should take no abuse from civilians and I should have had her arrested. He also gave the other soldier a severe dressing down for breaking confidence with a fellow soldier.

Unfortunately, the soldier was killed at Dieppe.

Throughout our continuous training we would dig slit trenches and string barbed wire. Quite often we were called out to fill bomb craters. At times while on guard duty on the English Channel at Winchelsea Beach, I would stare out to sea and imagine I could see invading boats coming in.

Training included firing all weapons and going on schemes and manoeuvres. I had fared fairly well at the ranges with the Bren gun, the Lewis gun, and the anti-tank rifle. However, firing the Lee Enfield rifle at 600 yards, I was all over the target. An officer came by and told the sergeant to check my rifle. He put five rounds into an area the size of a silver dollar. I was sent to the Fifteenth Canadian General Hospital at Bramshot for an eye test. The doctors at Bramshot wondered how I managed to get into an infantry regiment and told me I would have to transfer out.

While stationed at Eastbourne, my platoon officer, Lieutenant Ryerson, informed me that I would have to leave the regiment because of my poor eyesight. I said that under no condition was I leaving the regiment, the company, or the platoon: this was my home and my family. I liked the regiment and I intended to stay. On hearing this he went to the colonel. The colonel said to him that any man who feels that way about the regiment stays no matter what. I agreed to take over the two-inch mortar from Jack Stewart who had been promoted to lance-corporal, so the subject was dropped. It was hard to believe that among thousands of men it was so important that one who was handicapped with poor eyesight would not be equal to a German with good eyesight, therefore he might put himself and his comrades in jeopardy. This just proves that the Canadian army was thinking of the survival of its soldiers.

The regiment took part in many schemes and manoeuvres during our training in England. As they all had names, I still remember some of them. There was Bumper, Yukon, Tiger, and, of course, several others. The biggest manoeuvre that I was involved in was between Southern Command and Central Command. Literally tens of thousands of troops, guns, and tanks participated. At times we would go on manoeuvres with the British Home Guard, and act as the enemy. These blokes, armed with wooden rifles and broom handles, would always take this very seriously. During our training at Aldershot the Regiment was inspected by King George VI, Anthony Eden, and General Alan Brooke.

We were stationed in various places on the south coast of England: Lewes, Brighton, Winchelsea (twice), Ukfield, Eastbourne (twice), Hastings, Camberley, and Littlehampton. It was a good time to be alive with seven days leave every three months and a few weekends in London in between. It was great to share the perils of the war with the British people, and to visit my mother's relatives in Maidstone, Kent; Orpington, Kent; and Cheam, Surrey, and a few others in London where I was always made very welcome. I would visit the Beaver Club hoping to meet someone from home, and tour historical sites, such as Westminster Abbey, St. Paul's Cathedral, the Tower of London, and many other places. Canadians would generally spend a lot of time around Trafalgar Square and Picadilly.

I would also visit the little town of Addington, Surrey, where my mother was raised, and the neighbouring town of Croydon, which she often spoke of. I visited Croydon several times, and would pass through it on the train going in to London.

During the summer of 1941, while under canvas at a place called Hellingly, German planes came over and shot up the camp. However, the regiment was away on manoeuvres at the time. This was where my good friend Jim Mawbey got the sad news that his father had died, and where my buddy Red Perry suffered his wife's labour pains.

Before Christmas 1941, we were moved into a big estate owned by Sir Bernard Ekstein, a very wealthy man who had paid for a spitfire. We were in several rooms, and the servants were still employed. We were there for Christmas and it felt great to be in under cover for the winter. There was a pub a short distance away at a place called Fairwarp. Everything seemed to be working out fine until, shortly after Christmas, I suddenly came down with badly infected ears and, much to my regret, had to leave the regiment.

I pleaded with the medical officer, Captain Laird, to let me stay with the regiment and be treated there, but he told me that the infection was so bad I would have to be hospitalized.

I was first sent to the Fifth Casualty Clearing station at East Grinstead. The pain was so bad they could not really do much for me there, so I was sent by ambulance to the First Canadian General Hospital at Horsham. After several weeks of treatment I was discharged and sent on to Witley Camp against my wishes. This was where the reinforcements for the Second Division were.

On arrival at Witley Camp, I went directly to the orderly room to inquire about being returned to the regiment. Here I found a super chap, Company Sergeant-Major Norm MacIver. He sensed that I was concerned about the vigorous training that was going on there, and assured me that I would not be expected to take part in any of the training. In the meantime, all I would have to do was take care of the stove in the hut that I would be billeted in. During my stay at Witley Camp, I had two weekend passes to London and a midnight pass into Godalming every night of the week. However, I was desperate to get back to the regiment. Apparently, I had been overlooked when the next draft was being called out. The men that were on the draft were being inspected for venereal disease, lice, and crabs, before they were allowed to go. One man was found to have lice. A runner was sent to find me, and when he finally did, he told me that if I still wanted to go back to the regiment, I should grab my gear and get on the truck. On my arrival I was dropped off at "A" Company, as the companies were all in separate areas. It was my wish to go back to "D" Company. I contacted Company Sergeant-Major Murray that evening and told him that I belonged in "D" Company. He said: "We definitely want you back here, Poolton. Stay there tonight; we'll send the company truck to pick you up in the morning."

During this time, we were still waiting for the invasion of England — Operation Sea Lion. Meanwhile, the Germans had invaded Russia, making the invasion of England less likely to happen.

On May 18, 1942, we landed at Ryde on the Isle of Wight, where the strenuous training began that would prepare us for the upcoming Dieppe raid. We were asked if we could swim; I lied and told them I could.

Four

Operation Rutter

The Royal Regiment was billeted at Brambles Chine Holiday Camp, Fresh Water Bay, a great spot right on the beach. However, with all the strenuous training they were doing, they didn't have time to appreciate the locale.

After a heavy air raid on Portsmouth, several bombs were dropped on Cowes. The heavy anti-aircraft guns shook the whole island, and as we were in little cabins on the beach, Garth White, who was sleeping with his head under a sink, woke up with such a start that he hit his head on the sink and pulled it off the wall, breaking the water pipe. The following morning, many of us were sent to Cowes to dig out victims.

Part of our training would be rehearsals for landing. On one particular rehearsal, which took place on the coast of Devon, the British troops guarding that particular area had been told that we would be landing there in the early hours of the morning and not to open fire on anyone, as this was a practice landing. However, the Navy landed us three miles down the coast from where we were supposed to land and the troops in that area had not been told that there would be a landing taking place. We landed, were never challenged, and overran the positions being held by British troops in that area. They had no idea what was happening and, of course, we thought they knew we were coming. We took them totally by surprise. Lieutenant Ryerson immediately looked at his map and said, "We have landed in the wrong place. There should be a church steeple there [pointing]. We will have to double the three miles to the proper landing place." Lieutenant Ryerson told the British sergeant that they weren't doing a very good job of guarding and that we could have been Germans. The sergeant asked the officer if he was going to report him. Ryerson said, "No, but for Christ's sake, wake up man. This is your country." That was the end of that. We doubled the three miles to the next town, where we were supposed to have landed.

The US Rangers that trained with us were amazed at the type of training we were doing. They would tell us that their troops had an awful lot of catching up to do.

On July 2, after completing several landing rehearsals on the coast of Devon, the regiment embarked on H.M.S. *Princess Josephine Charlotte* and H.M.S. *Princess Astrid*. When the regiment was aboard, Lieutenant-Colonel Basher announced that this was not an exercise, but an actual operation against the enemy. The troops let out a great cheer.

We were to have no identification whatsoever (with the exception of identification disks): no pay books, cigarette packages, photographs, or any other items.

General Roberts visited the ships and made the same announcement Basher had made. On Friday, July 3, Lord Mountbatten visited all vessels in the convoy announcing that Operation Rutter against Dieppe would begin at 04:30 hours the next morning. Weather conditions forced a twenty-four-hour postponement.

After the troops had been on board ship for four days, we went ashore on July 6 for a two-hour route march, and then re-embarked. At approximately 06:00 hours on July 7, four German Focke Wulf 190 Fighter Bombers swept in low over the channel and attacked the *Princess Josephine Charlotte* and the *Princess Astrid* with five-hundred-pound bombs, hitting them directly. It was hard to believe that these bombs passed through both ships before exploding. Only four minor casualties were suffered by the Royals, but several of the ships crew were killed. An "abandon ship" order was given, as the ship I was on was sinking. The Royals boarded their landing craft and were taken ashore to the Isle of Wight. Operation Rutter was cancelled for all time.

Five
Operation Jubilee

The troops were disappointed when General Roberts told them that Operation Rutter was cancelled. They had been all keyed up and looking forward to having a go at the Germans.

After several weeks of vigorous training that consisted of forced marches, cliff scaling, practice landings from the sea, unarmed combat, demolition, and the firing of all weapons from the hip, the cancellation of Operation Rutter meant the troops of the Canadian Second Division (Simmer Force) would return to the mainland. Upon return the Royals were stationed at Five Oaks under canvas. While there, most of the regiment was sent on seven days' leave. I decided to go to Birmingham and while there did not mention Dieppe to anyone at any time.

I was enjoying myself in Birmingham and had forgotten all about what we had been doing. There I met Irene Fox, a lassie from Lancashire who was in the Women's Auxiliary Air Force (W.A.A.F.), stationed on a balloon site at Hall Green. We both arrived at New Street station in Birmingham around 22:00 hours on the same train while there was an air raid on. As all transportation had stopped due to the air raid, we spent the remainder of the night down under the station, which served as a shelter. Being the only two that were in uniform, we struck up a conversation. She told me she was coming back from seven days' leave and had to be in by midnight and was worried about getting into trouble. I told her that I would go with her and explain to her sergeant why she was late. The sergeant, who was very nice, said there was no problem and thanked me. As I had already asked Irene for a date, before leaving I asked the sergeant if she could have a midnight pass. Irene stood there, almost dumfounded, waiting for the answer. The sergeant agreed that she could have a pass until midnight.

We toured the city of Birmingham. It was a pleasure to be with her and although we talked about many things she would not talk about the balloon. I promised to see her on my next leave and we exchanged letters. She gave me her hat badge as something to remember her by. I also received a letter from her mother, who ran a pub and told me that the beer would be on the house whenever I came to visit. I am sorry to say that the Dieppe operation put an end to all this. I never saw Irene again.

During my many trips to Birmingham on leave, I could never pay for a bus or tram fare. They wouldn't take the money. It was the same in the pubs. Before I could get my money out, a civilian would be paying for my beer. (However, it was not like that in London.) When my seven day leaves were coming to an end, I would always say my goodbyes before leaving for the train, as I could not bear to see the tearful goodbyes of mothers and wives at the station.

Shortly after my return to Five Oaks, we were suddenly moved to Littlehampton on the channel coast. There we relieved the First Canadian Division, Forty-Eighth Highlanders, and settled in to what we all thought would be a great place to be billeted. At first we were not as popular as the Highlanders, who were very well liked by the people. However, this did not last.

On the first Sunday there, two German F.W. 190s came in very low over the channel and dropped five-hundred-pound bombs, one a direct hit on a cinema that killed and injured a lot of innocent children. The second plane dropped its bomb on a huge pyramid-shaped cement obstacle that was on the coast as part of a tank barrier.

This explosion blew several of us back into the doorway of our billets, breaking all of the windows on the main street. It also demolished "A" Company's cook house. Jim Mawbey was standing guard about twenty-five yards away. I remember Red Perry saying "the bastard got Jim." But, to our relief, Jim appeared unscathed. The attack lasted only a few minutes before the planes went back across the channel. We could see the pilot sitting in the cockpit as he banked the aircraft before leaving. This all seemed very strange.

First they bombed the Royals' two ships off the Isle of Wight and now they were after us in Littlehampton. It looked like the Germans knew something was in the wind.

Several of us had contracted trench mouth (infection of the gums) while on the Isle of Wight. This was the result of washing our mess tins in filthy water. We received treatment for the trench mouth from a Canadian dentist. While returning from our third treatment for this disease, we stopped at an English tearoom. There were about eight of us from my platoon, and we sat enjoying tea and pastries and talking about the army and girls. This was a great time in my life. Later on, this stop would become a recurring memory for me.

Arriving back at the billets, we found everybody busy checking weapons and ammunition. Lieutenant Ryerson, my platoon officer, told me that we were going on a manoeuvre and to be sure to take both smoke and H.E. (high explosive) bombs for the two-inch mortar. My number-two man, Private Wilson, refused to carry any of the H.E., so it was decided that he would carry the twelve smoke bombs and I would carry the twelve H.E. in my haversack on my back. I decided then that this was something other than just another manoeuvre, and I had better keep a low profile as I was being treated for trench mouth and might not be allowed to go.

I regretted that our stay in Littlehampton was going to be so brief. It was a beautiful town with tearooms, restaurants, and, of course, pubs.

Shortly after lunch, we received an order to be out on the street with all arms and equipment in fifteen minutes. We were hustled into waiting trucks. The tarps were tied down across the back, something we had never had done before.

Immediately the trucks moved off, carrying the Royals to Portsmouth, where we were driven into the dock yards. The troops then embarked on two troop carriers, the *Queen Emma* and the *Princess Astrid*. "D" and "C" Companies embarked on the *Queen Emma*.

Once aboard the ship, I was told by one of the sailors that we were headed for Dieppe. Apparently, the raid had been resurrected and it was now called Operation Jubilee. The troop carriers were being disguised as merchant vessels. False funnels and bulkheads had been erected to alter their appearance, and flags of neutral countries were being flown.

Two hundred and thirty seven ships of all types were leaving England's shores that night. After dark and out of the sight of land, the flags and the false funnels were lowered, exposing the ALCs (Assault Landing Craft) that were to carry the Royals to the beaches of Dieppe. The last thing I remember seeing as we slipped away was Nelson's ship, the H.M.S. *Victory*.

It was surprising that we were allowed to carry items of identification such as shoulder flashes, pay books, money, letters, and cigarettes. For Operation Rutter, we had been stripped of all these items.

After having a meal we immediately got busy listening to lectures and studying aerial photographs and maps, which later proved obsolete. While trying to picture in our minds what we might expect to encounter during the landings, we were very calm, almost as if we were on manoeuvres. Being dedicated to the task ahead and having trained very hard we were eager to see action and prove ourselves good soldiers. We were told we would not need respirators, and water bottles would be optional; it was thought that we would not need them as we would only be in France a few hours. On the ship, sandwiches and tea were made available, but went mostly untouched. There was no rum ration given, and no praying. We were going into our first action cold.

Each man had to go out on deck to prime his two grenades. This was a ticklish job to do particularly in the dark and on a moving ship. Every one was normal; there was no sign of tension. We were told that we could write a letter home and note at the top "to be mailed only if I fail to return." The letters would go back to England with the mother ship.

It was a beautiful and peaceful night. The channel was as calm as a mill pond. We had mine sweepers ahead as the channel was heavily mined, and were hoping that the Navy would land us at our proper destination. When the time finally came to transfer to the landing craft, we went in single file through the dark in silence, holding onto the bayonet scabbard of the man ahead. We were helped across a three-foot space by two naval ratings (sailors) into the ALCs. They were then lowered into the sea and we bade farewell to the mother ship and headed for the coast of France.

TO BE MAILED ONLY IF I FAIL TO RETURN

Mrs. Thomas Poolton,
Box 64,
Kapuskasing, Ontario

August 18, 1942

Dear Mum,

I am writing this letter on board the troop carrier, H.M.S. *Queen Emma*. We are finally going to see action, and at present are heading for Dieppe, a German held port on the French coast. This is going to be a frontal attack using infantry and tanks. We are to capture and hold for four hours and then withdraw and embark for England. There are hundreds of ships taking part in this operation. Everyone is calm, almost the same as when on manoeuvres, but eager to come to grips with the enemy. I only hope that we are as good as our fathers were in the Great War. I feel very proud of my regiment and have confidence in the officers and men. I hope they have confidence in me. I am the two-inch-mortar man for 16 Platoon. I have just finished priming my grenades out on deck in the dark. This is a tricky job and has to be done away from the other men for safety. I keep thinking that this is just another manoeuvre except that we are preparing all our weapons for action and will be firing them in anger tomorrow. The English Channel is very calm tonight, just like a mill pond. Our landing craft are hanging where the life boats would normally be. It is a very beautiful and peaceful night. We feel honoured that the Second Canadian Division was chosen for this operation, but it all depends on how good our security is. We must have the benefit of surprise and the cover of darkness or we will be at a disadvantage. We all know that the enemy has well-trained and experienced soldiers, but we volunteered and trained very hard for this and would not want to miss it under any condition. I am sure that the ship's crew will get us to our destination safely. We have mine sweepers ahead of us as the channel is heavily mined. As you have told me many times, being born with a veil is a sign that I will never drown.

I know that your thoughts and prayers will be with me tomorrow on August 19th.

God Bless You All,

Your Loving Son, Jack

Jack Poolton B67587
"D" Company
Royal Regiment of Canada

The beach at Puys, France, where the Royal Regiment landed on August 19, 1942.

Six

Blue Beach

At approximately 04:00 hours and still several miles from the French coast, gunfire suddenly erupted to our left. We knew the British Third Commando was to our left, but could not understand why there should be any firing this far from their target.

As it turned out, a German convoy heading for the port of Dieppe had intercepted Third Commando's landing craft. They attacked, sinking some and scattering others, resulting in some of the commandos returning to England. The remainder continued on and eventually reached their target.

Our escort ships engaged the convoy, resulting in heavy gun fire, leaving one of their ships ablaze. At one point, the Royals' flotilla was so close that I could make out figures on one of the German ships.

The Royals had to turn in circles for over twenty minutes to avoid detection. As there was total radio silence, we had no way of contacting the headquarters' ship to report this. The delay would cause the Royals to land later than planned.

Finally, the convoy cleared the area and the Royals continued on. The Germans on shore, having been alerted, fired star shells and chandelier flares that lit up the channel, exposing our landing craft and escort vessels.

Dawn was breaking and the Royals were still two miles out at sea. We needed the element of surprise and the cover of darkness to penetrate the German defences and advance inland, but now it appeared that we would be landing twenty to twenty-five minutes late and in full daylight.

Suddenly, all hell broke loose. The sky lit up like a giant display of fireworks. It sounded like a thousand guns firing. Squadrons of twin-engine bombers were going in very low but failed to hit any of the coastal defences. The first wave of Royals finally hit the beach at 05:07 hours. It should have been 04:45 hours. The order was now given for the second wave to land.

Within approximately five hundred yards of the beach we came under heavy machine gun and mortar fire. The bullets hitting the hull of the landing craft sounded like hail on a tin roof.

The armour-piercing rounds easily penetrated the landing craft's hull. One of them pierced the shoulder of my tunic as well as the tunic of a man across from me and went out the other side, without touching flesh. All I felt was a tug as the round pierced my tunic.

In my landing craft, the men were still very calm but tension was rising. I could feel the heartbeat of the man next to me. This was not from fear but anticipation of the task ahead. The second wave was to advance inland after the first had broken through the defences. However, this was to prove impossible as the first wave had run into a maelstrom of machine-gun and mortar fire and many were killed or wounded in the first few minutes of landing on the beach.

As we landed we were under a continuous stream of heavy machine-gun and mortar fire and as the ramp was dropped the firing came straight into the landing craft.

We had landed directly in front of a machine gun. There was no hesitation as the second wave hit the beach. Being the two-inch-mortar man and part of platoon headquarters, I was one of the last out, along with Lieutenant Ryerson.

It seemed that within seconds of the ramp going down, they had put the landing craft in reverse and were backing out. I jumped off the ramp into about eight feet of water. I was carrying a heavy load that included not only the two-inch mortar, but also twelve high-explosive mortar bombs, two hand grenades and 250 rounds of 303 ammunition.

As I hit the water, the mortar slipped off my shoulder. I bent down and was able to run my arm through the sling and retrieve it. This delay caused me to lose track of the platoon. I staggered up the beach with a machine gun kicking up the stones at my feet. I still wonder how he missed me. I recall seeing several dead lying on the ramp, one being my good friend Ray Lloyd.

As the smoke screen was clearing I emerged aghast at the carnage before me, and I knew I had landed in hell.

I heard a voice yell, "Run, Poolton!" As I turned to go to the right I could see a tank turret that was built into the wall. I threw myself down beside a shallow abutment, hoping it would give me some cover.

The Germans were dropping mortars every twenty to thirty feet up the beach. I tilted my helmet to shield my eyes as one bomb had landed very close. I could not believe how accurate they were with these mortars. It was as though it had all been rehearsed.

A sniper hit the rim of my helmet, almost knocking it off my head. I guess I was lucky he did not hit the haversack that contained the 12 two-inch mortar bombs.

I could hear the bullets hitting the dead bodies around me. Men were trying to throw hand grenades through the slits of the blockhouse where the machine gun was firing from, but they were being hit just as they had pulled the pin. The grenade would then explode among our own men. Others were desperately firing Bren guns and the anti-tank rifle at the slits hoping to hit the German machine gunners, but as one was hit they would drag him out, and another would immediately take his place. (Later, when I made trips back to the beach with a German stretcher to pick up wounded, I was able to see the dead Germans lying behind the blockhouse!)

There was a signal man trying desperately to contact the destroyer, which was off Blue Beach, to request that they fire three or four shells from their four-inch guns to knock a hole in the wall so that the men could get through. There was no reply, not one shell was fired from the sea that day to assist the Royals. I wondered why the destroyer was there at all. Sadly, I witnessed the bombing and sinking of this destroyer, H.M.S. *Berkley* later that day.

I had lost contact with Private Wilson with the smoke bombs and had not seen him since leaving the mother ship. As there was no way to fire high-explosive bombs without endangering our own men, I dropped the mortar and bombs and picked up the nearest rifle with the intention of scaling the cliff. I had observed that men were slowly climbing up, hugging the cliff, underneath the barbed wire. They had not yet been detected by any of the snipers. The man ahead of me had just reached the summit when he was hit and killed instantly. He slid down, taking me with him to the bottom. The Germans then kept this area under close observation, and no one else made it to the top.

The Germans started dropping hand grenades from the top of the cliff, causing our people to try to throw our grenades with a four-second fuse up and over the top. The result was that the grenades came back down, exploding on the way, adding to our problems.

With the tide coming in, some of the wounded were drowning. One landing craft made it to shore and was taking out wounded. The Germans dropped a mortar shell inside the landing craft, causing it to sink. I recall seeing the wounded being machine-gunned as they were clinging to the sinking craft.

It appeared that no further rescue attempts would be possible at Blue Beach. After ignoring two orders to surrender, someone put his undershirt up on a bayonet. It was then apparent that the Royals had decided to surrender.

Captain Housser, my company commander, turned to me and said, "I am not going to surrender."

I replied, "Neither am I, sir."

We both knew that there were no reinforcements coming. We were entirely on our own.

The two of us and a third man, whose name I did not know, took off along the beach in the direction of Dieppe armed with rifles. On the way we suddenly came under fire from a machine gun mounted on the end of a pier. We were trapped and forced to return.

On arriving back, we discovered German soldiers down on the beach. I observed some of our men attempting to put grenades with the pin pulled under dead bodies, hoping to get the Germans when they were moved. I cautioned that it might not be Germans that would be removing the bodies.

We found out later that while capturing Canadian soldiers, the Germans also captured the plans for the raid.

Seven

Captivity

There was no way to escape the inevitable. The Germans were on three sides, the English Channel on the other. If the men continued to resist. It would only mean more bloodshed. The Royals' medical officer, Captain Laird, was seriously wounded. The tide had begun to come in and the wounded lying on the beach were drowning. These brave men now knew that victory was impossible. In all the noise and confusion, Jack heard a voice yell, "Sir, they're demanding that we surrender." The answer was, "Tell them to go to hell." Finally, it was realized that it was futile to resist any longer. The white flag had been hoisted. Reluctantly, the Royals had begun to surrender. Slowly the murderers who had not yet been seen emerged from everywhere. They yelled orders of "hande hock!" (hands up). Then they ordered the prisoners to throw all their weapons and helmets into a pile. If only they'd been given the chance to fight!

Captain Housser, myself, and another man were the last to drop our weapons and surrender on Blue Beach. A tremendous feeling of humiliation set in. With everything we had against us and even though we felt as if we had been wasted, the men continued to act as soldiers. I was proud of the conduct of our men, both Canadian and British. You can train a soldier to fight and you can train a soldier to accept death, but there is no way to prepare a soldier to be taken prisoner. The experience can only be understood by one who has been through the humiliation.

Prisoners Of War

Private Jack Poolton, Royal Regiment of Canada, is a prisoner of war in Germany, according to a cable received by his parents, Mr. and Mrs. Tom Poolton of Kapuskasing, from the International Red Cross. He joined the Royals in April, 1940, and was in Iceland with his unit. In the Dieppe raid Pte. Poolton was reported missing, and his parents said that they had almost given up hope when the report came saying he was a prisoner. He was the second to join up in Kapuskasing. He has a brother serving at Camp Borden.

Pte. Joseph Russell Wil-

Pte. J. Poolton

Newspaper clippings from the *Toronto Telegram* reporting that Jack had been captured in the Dieppe raid.

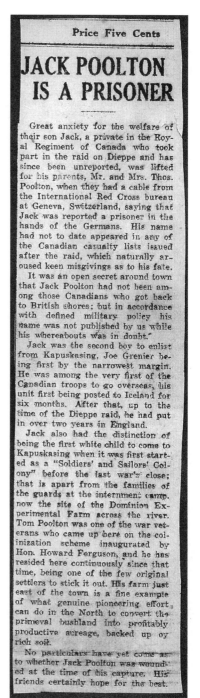

Price Five Cents

JACK POOLTON IS A PRISONER

Great anxiety for the welfare of their son Jack, a private in the Royal Regiment of Canada who took part in the raid on Dieppe and has since been unreported, was lifted for his parents, Mr. and Mrs. Thos. Poolton, when they had a cable from the International Red Cross bureau at Geneva, Switzerland, saying that Jack was reported a prisoner in the hands of the Germans. His name had not to date appeared in any of the Canadian casualty lists issued after the raid, which naturally aroused keen misgivings as to his fate.

It was an open secret around town that Jack Poolton had not been among those Canadians who got back to British shores; but in accordance with defined military policy his name was not published by us while his whereabouts was in doubt."

Jack was the second boy to enlist from Kapuskasing, Joe Grenier being first by the narrowest margin. He was among the very first of the Canadian troops to go overseas, his unit first being posted to Iceland for six months. After that, up to the time of the Dieppe raid, he had put in over two years in England.

Jack also had the distinction of being the first white child to come to Kapuskasing when it was first started as a "Soldiers' and Sailors' Colony" before the last war's close; that is apart from the families of the guards at the internment camp, now the site of the Dominion Experimental Farm across the river. Tom Poolton was one of the war veterans who came up here on the colinization scheme inaugurated by Hon. Howard Ferguson, and he has resided here continuously since that time, being one of the few original settlers to stick it out. His farm just east of the town is a fine example of what genuine pioneering effort can do in the North to convert the primeval bushland into profitably productive acreage, backed up by rich soil.

No particulars have yet come as to whether Jack Poolton was wounded at the time of his capture. His friends certainly hope for the best.

A German officer speaking English asked, "What took you so long? We have been waiting for you for ten days." The Germans then forced us up a ladder that had been lowered over the wall. As we began to climb the ladder, the man at the very top was accidentally pushed from behind. The German soldier at the top of the ladder shot the man who had been pushed. A German senior officer came on the scene and shot the German. We were shocked to see an officer shoot one of his own men!

I volunteered with several others to return to the beach to try to rescue some of the badly wounded from the rising tide. The Germans had not ordered us to rescue the men, but we wanted to save them from drowning — even if it meant that they would become prisoners also. I was able to make three trips with German stretchers before we were stopped. There were pieces of bodies everywhere, corpses with the whites of their eyes transfixed on the heavens. The water had turned a sickly pink colour, and the air was filled with the sweet smell of blood and death and cordite. There were arms and legs, and boots with feet in them everywhere. The stones were stained with blood and there were men still burning, stuck in the barbed wire with packs of explosives on their backs. It was heart-wrenching to see this terrible destruction of human bodies and to see the blue patch of the Second Division — which we were all so proud of — ripped, torn, and stained with blood.

I looked up as I bent down to speak to a wounded man and saw a German officer walking from place to place shooting the worst of the wounded in the head to put them out of their misery. I suppose it was an act of mercy on his part, but it infuriated me! These were my comrades. Days before we had laughed and joked, and here I was witnessing their murders!

The Germans were still firing at dead bodies that had washed out into the channel. Was it not enough that they had killed these men? Did they have to riddle them with bullets for hours afterwards?

The prisoners were herded into columns and marched into Puys where we were temporarily held in a school courtyard. A German stood guard on top of the high stone wall. Seconds later an allied aircraft flying at rooftop level and not knowing that the men inside were Canadian, flew over with guns blazing. He managed to hit the German, but also hit five Canadians. I watched as the blood of five comrades ran into one large pool in the middle of the cement floor. What surprised me was that the blood was five different shades of red. Later that day, we were marched through the town of Dieppe to the Hôtel Dieu (the Dieppe hospital). We witnessed a soldier from the Black Watch putting a field dressing on a pregnant French woman who had been shot through the stomach. She was left sitting on a chair out in the open. The Germans had completely ignored her.

All along the road on both sides from Puys to Dieppe, there were German soldiers standing in holes. All you could see were their eyes and part of their helmets. We used slit trenches, the American's used foxholes, and now it was apparent that the German's used what looked to me like holes for telephone poles. Some will still say that the Germans were not expecting us, but obviously they hadn't dug these holes the day of the raid.

The badly wounded were taken into the hospital, where they were tended by the Nuns of the Communaute des Augustines. Those of us who remained outside were ordered to throw down all valuables. The booty consisted of paybooks, rings, watches, money, pocketknives, and fountain pens. I was able to hide a ring that my father had given me before I left to go overseas. It was something he had worn in the First World War. I also managed to hide my paybook inside my tunic pocket. However, my wallet and other valuables were confiscated.

Up until this time, the Royals did not know what had happened to the rest of the units. At Dieppe we were shocked to learn that the other units had suffered the same fate on the other beaches. Now all hope was lost.

It was tragic. If only we had landed like we had trained, using stealth and the cover of darkness like the British did. Over the years, the Canadians have been accused of being "un-tried" and "un-blooded," but we could have accomplished as much or maybe more than the commandos if we had been given the right conditions. Instead, the Canadians were landed en masse on open beaches in daylight under severe machine-gun fire and mortars and with no supporting fire. However, the more experienced British were not under Canadian command. I decided then that those who planned this disaster had to be idiots.

Later that afternoon of the 19th, they marched us out in fives to Envermeu some fourteen kilometres away. Some of the men had lost their shoes. Several had shed their uniforms in the water to make it easier to swim. French women had tried to offer the men a drink of water, but the Germans tipped over their buckets and chased the women away. German photographers were busy taking pictures of the prisoners with hands held high in the air. These photographs would be used as propaganda — evidence that Churchill's second front was "kaput."

When we reached the outskirts of Dieppe, a single voice started to hum the "Marseillaise." Within a few minutes the entire column was singing the anthem loudly. The infuriated Germans tried to put a stop to it, but were unsuccessful. The French civilians wept and showed the men the "V" sign for victory as they watched these proud soldiers, now prisoners, who had travelled so far from home to try to help them. German officers on horseback rode into the crowd trying to disperse them, but to no avail. A few minutes later we were whistling "The Maple Leaf Forever," but that didn't seem to bother the Germans as many of them had never heard the tune and did not realize what it meant to us.

One French woman came alongside the men. She whispered to a soldier of the Royal Hamilton Light Infantry to curse her in French. As the soldier began to shake his fist at her and shout obscenities in French, she began throwing tomatoes at him and some of the others, pretending to be pelting them in anger. The tomatoes were caught and hidden inside the men's tunics to be consumed at a later time. The Germans found this insanely funny and patted the woman on the back, praising her for flinging tomatoes at the *Englander schwein*.

Truckloads of German troops were passing us, heading for Dieppe, all flying the Union Jack to protect them from our aircraft. I wondered where they got all those Union Jacks.

The Germans had rewarded the French people for their good conduct during the raid by sending all their POWs home. This, of course, was done for propaganda purposes.

We passed a signpost along the way which told us that we were six kilometres away from Envermeu. We passed a wedding party, the bride in her wedding gown and veil, the groom in his suit. This was Monsieur and Mme. Paul Dupuis, who had just been married at L'Eglise d'Envermeu. The wedding party stopped and watched the prisoners march by. The bride cried as the men began to throw money to her. (Mme. Dupuis kept a penny as a souvenir of this day, and showed it to us years later when myself and other veterans made a pilgrimage to Dieppe.) The best man,

Monsieur Robillard, saw that the feet of one of the prisoners, Stan Darch, were cut and bleeding. He bent down and unlaced his new brown shoes and handed them to Darch, much to the prisoner's surprise. Monsieur Robillard was seized by the Germans and imprisoned.

Later, some friendly French women arrived with cans of milk. The men closest to the women were lucky enough to get some milk to quench their thirst, but the women had another motive in mind. As the Germans rode right into the crowd, trying to stop the men from getting to the milk and creating a lot of confusion, the French women passed skirts and blouses to several of the French-Canadian prisoners, who quickly donned the outfits and successfully escaped with the women. Fortunately, the guards did not notice the army boots underneath the skirts.

The officers were separated from the enlisted men and led into an old church where they were to spend the night. The aged priest welcomed them, handing each a handful of straw to use as a pillow. He was surprised at how well the French-Canadians spoke his language. He told them that the Germans had been waiting for them for three weeks.

As for the rest of us, when we finally reached Envermeu we were exhausted. We were herded into an unfinished clock factory with a dirt floor. By this time, the German soldiers had been replaced by Hitler Youth, an arrogant and sadistic group, who showed the exhausted prisoners that they meant business and would kill anyone who tried to escape. That first night will remain in my mind forever. Dying of thirst, I had scraped a hole in the dirt floor and pressed my tongue and parched lips to the damp earth. After having been over my head in salt water, my thirst was overwhelming, as we had had nothing to drink since leaving the mother ship and most of the men were not carrying water bottles. I don't really know how I made it through that night. With thoughts of conditions getting even worse, I decided that it was worth risking my life to try to escape.

The walking wounded had not been attended to and their wounds were starting to become infected. Morale was low and our defeat had started to sink in. Suddenly, a voice sounded out of the darkness. A man, short in stature, stood before us. It was Regimental Sergeant Major Harry Beesley of the British Third Commando. He began to organize the men, telling us to place the wounded in a separate corner of the building. He instructed us to divide evenly the meager rations of bread that had been handed out. But most importantly, he gave us a "pep" talk, telling us that, at all times, we must conduct ourselves as soldiers. We must always show the Germans our bravery. Although we had lost the battle on the beaches after courageously fighting, our fight was not finished. We had to survive.

The next morning, we were awakened at 06:00 hours and given a small piece of black bread before our long march to a French prison camp at a place called Verneulles.

Eight
Train Ride to Hell

On the fifth day, at Verneulles, the Dieppe prisoners were marched to a train siding at Verneulles, where they were herded like cattle into boxcars (cattle trucks). These cars were a lot smaller than North American cars and had a small opening in either end for ventilation. Although the cars were labelled "40 hommes, 8 chevaux" (forty men or eight horses), fifty men were to be put in each car. The number of men was kept to exactly fifty so that the German soldiers, who would do a head count, would know if any prisoners had escaped en route to Germany. Jack had searched out his friend George Pelletier, who could speak French fluently. At the same time, George was searching for Jack with the same idea in mind: escape. They found each other in the midst of hundreds of prisoners, ready to be loaded into these cars. They decided to head for a car from which they thought they could escape.

The camp at Verneulles was a nightmare. It had this unforgettable stench that I have never encountered since. Everything about the camp was revolting. The gallows were stark and formidable, and food was almost nonexistent, so we ate grass and some of the weeds. The Vichy French government tried to drive a wedge between the francophones and the anglophones by giving cigarettes, food, and biscuits to the French-Canadians and giving them the opportunity to talk on the radio to their homes in Canada. The Germans had told them that, as France was not at war with Germany and they were French, they shouldn't be at war either. A French-Canadian officer told the Germans that we were all Canadians and that Canada was at war with Germany. He told his men to accept the offering but to share it with the anglophones. My mind went back to the last thing I had enjoyed in England: the tea and pastries we stopped for on our way back to camp from our trench-mouth treatment. How my heart ached to be back in England.

After experiencing the terrible camp at Verneulles, I had decided I could not handle the fact that I was a prisoner and, with the thought of conditions getting even worse, I knew I had to escape as soon as possible. George Pelletier and I pledged to each other that we would escape from the train, risking death to ourselves or to anyone that got in our way. We reasoned that a successful escape had to be made while on French soil, as Pelletier speak French fluently. We hoped to cross France to Spain, unless by a stroke of luck we could contact the French underground.

"Ten will be shot for every one that escapes!" was being screamed at us by a German officer speaking English. With these words ringing in my ears and one particular car in sight, George and I dodged from one group of fifty men to another, trying to reach it. This car had an opening that was about three feet long and one foot wide, with 2 three-quarter-inch steel bars across and barbed wire on the outside. Other cars had a solid-steel grating bolted across the opening which had small openings about an inch in diameter, which would have made it impossible to get out. Finally, amidst the kicks and rifle butts, we managed to get to the car we had picked out. After being pushed through the door and treading on wounded men, we immediately made for the end of the car. We had finally made it into the one that we hoped we could escape from! I breathed a sigh of relief.

The train was very long, and was pulled by five locomotives. "Churchill's Second Front Kaput" and "Gangster Schwein" were painted in huge white letters the full length of the train. The German people had been told that the Canadians were actually convicts that had been let out of prison to participate in the raid on Dieppe. If we were successful, we were to be pardoned. Of course, this propaganda was passed on to the French people as well in order to poison them against us.

We were crowded in the car shoulder to shoulder. There was no room to lie down, so we either had to stand or squat. We were given a round loaf of black bread about ten inches in diameter as well as another sixth of a loaf. The bread was to last us five days, although we did not know this at the time. There was no water to quench our thirst. A large wooden tub sat in the centre of the car to be used as a latrine. The air in the car was foul. Men's wounds developed maggots, and the stench was overpowering, the hot weather only made the smell worse. The air vents were not large enough to let in sufficient fresh air.

Finally the train started to move and we began to get ready for the escape. We had decided to eat the smaller portion of bread, and shoved the full loaf around to the back of our tunics, expecting that we might land on our chest, and it might injure us. We discovered that two British commandos had the same idea, so we teamed up. As darkness fell, with a superhuman effort, the four of us spread the bars wide enough to get one of the commandos out to unfasten the door. He was small in stature with a flat chest. We pushed him out of the opening and in his bare feet, he clung with his fingers and toes to the moving train, which was swaying dangerously at high speed. We stood there, hardly daring to breathe, waiting to hear a shot as there were Germans with machine guns on top of every second car. We could see their shadows in the moonlight. After a few minutes of dead silence, there was a tap at the door. The commando had twisted the lock off with a small bar that he had picked up along the railway, and had concealed it down his pant leg. We forced the sliding door back enough to let him in. This act of bravery by this man should have been rewarded. It was one of the many I witnessed during my time as a POW.

We would have to jump at intervals and hope that we would land in one piece and unnoticed by the Germans. I stood looking out the open door, my heart pounding. I had lowered myself down and let my feet touch the railway ties, but pulled back as the train seemed to be picking up speed. The moon was full — almost as bright as day — casting a shadow that would have been to our advantage. We had hoped that there would be some cover, such as bushes or trees, but there was nothing but wheat fields for miles. I kept thinking over and over, "Would the Germans really shoot ten men for every one that escaped?" I could not get this out of my mind. That would mean forty men. And would they shoot wounded men? We told the other men in the car that, after we had left, anyone would be free to leave.

The tension was mounting. If we were going to make a break, it had to be now! The only way that we could leave the moving train was to somersault out with arms folded trying not to break an arm or a leg upon landing. Both Pelletier and myself, having escaped both death and wounds on the beach, believed that it was our duty to ourselves and to our regiment to escape.

Then things began to happen in the car. Several men were putting their boots back on, preparing to follow us. We heard a voice in the darkness say, "You will get us all shot. Stay in the car!" We ignored it, until a Canadian sergeant stood up and ordered us not to leave the car. All hell broke loose. The two commandos turned on the sergeant saying he was a disgrace to his regiment. One commando attempted to pull the stripes from the sergeant's sleeve. I tried to pull Pelletier away and get off the train. A fellow Royal from "D" Company was putting on his boots, sitting at the edge of the door waiting for us to leave. Meanwhile, the train was travelling closer and closer towards Paris. The Germans wanted as many people as possible to see this train with its precious cargo of prisoners.

After reaching the outskirts of Paris, the train suddenly began to slow down. We thought this was our chance, but it was not. The train stopped alongside a passenger train full of people, mostly German officers. We had to close the door. They were staring at the words painted on the side of the train. The moment we had come to a full stop, and just as we were about to make a move, we noticed German soldiers on both sides of the train examining the doors. They discovered that the lock on our door was missing and the door had been tampered with. They flung back the door and counted the men to see if there were still fifty in the car. We had replaced the barbed wire and they did not notice that the bars had been spread. There was a lot of screaming and shouting outside and a French railway worker, who was working nearby, was seized and taken away, accused of unlocking the door!

This was a terrible blow. I honestly believed if Pelletier and myself could have got off the train safely, we would have made it back to the safety of England and our regiment. My heart sank. I was numb. We were so close: door opened, looking out at all those fields and open countryside. I stood and uttered every curse I knew. Over and over and over I cursed, until I was almost exhausted. It seemed that fate was against us that night.

Once again the train started to move, faster and faster, rolling steadily on toward Germany. I dreaded the crossing of the German border and started planning another escape, although we had pretty well given up any idea of getting off the train.

At a stop in France, there were women with a cart of fruit waiting on the station platform with the intention of giving the fruit to the prisoners. The Germans fell upon them, tipping their carts over. They stomped on the fruit and used rifle butts on the women. A man threw some tobacco rolled up in a piece of newspaper. He had thrown this from twenty feet away, missing the barbed wire on the outside. I caught it as it came through the opening.

The weather was hot, night and day. By about the third day in the car, the latrine bucket was overflowing. The straw that was on the floor contained cow manure, fleas, and several other types of insects. Conditions were getting worse and life was getting grimmer as the days went by. Most of the men had finished their bread, and we still had two more days to go.

When we had finally crossed the dreaded German border, there were soldiers galore and trains passing us, loaded with tanks and guns. Unlike England, the names of the towns had not been removed from the station platforms. There was something alien about the sound of the train wheels hitting the joints of the rails. The Canadian trains made a "clickety-click" sound. The German trains made a simple "click-click." This was due to the fact that the joints on the German rails were directly across from one another, whereas in Canada they were staggered.

After five days and nights the train came to a stop at a place called Lamsdorf. The doors were flung open — what a relief after being in there all that time. We blindly staggered out of the cars as we descended from darkness into daylight. After our eyes had adjusted to the light, we were horrified to see Russian prisoners, mere skeletons wearing rags, unloading an ammunition train. Guards were carrying bullwhips, which they did not hesitate to use, as well as rifles and revolvers. I thought, "My God — they would have to shoot me before they'll use a bullwhip on me." What a shock, after all we'd been through and all we'd witnessed — a stark preamble to what was about to follow.

Nine
Life at Stalag VIIIB

The men were formed into columns for the mile-long march to the prison camp. They marched down a road lined with cherry trees. Although the men were weak with hunger, they had been warned by the guards that they would be shot for picking any of the cherries.

Further down the road they passed a cemetery filled with small dirty black crosses stretching as far as the eye could see. As the men neared the crosses, they discovered that these were not German graves, but were the resting places of Allied prisoners from the First World War who had died during their incarceration by the Germans.

As the Canadians approached the gates of Stalag VIIIB, they lifted their heads proudly, marching as if on parade: all in step, all in line. They marched toward the gates singing "The Yanks are Coming." The British prisoners, many of which had been captured at Dunkirk, yelled "Good old Canada," and cheered the defeated men.

We were stopped outside the gates for searches, registration, and counting. We were then photographed, fingerprinted, and issued a disk with our *Kriegsgefangener* number. I was given disk number 26212.

When being registered, most of the men said their occupation was farming. A German officer was heard to say, "my, they have an awful lot of farmers in Canada."

The only thing that seemed to be in our favour was the

weather, which was almost beautiful the day we arrived at Stalag VIIIB — though standing out in the hot sun was a little hard to bear in our weakened state. Finally, after the searches and counts, we were marched up through the main street of the Stalag.

There were compounds on either sides of the road, and, to our amazement, these chaps who had been captured at Dunkirk and other places were cheering us. Being a defeated lot and having these chaps cheer us actually did something to us: it lifted our spirits. One lad with a New Zealand accent yelled, "Are there any Kiwis out there?" A voice from behind me replied, "What the hell are Kiwis?" (We found out later that the word "Kiwi" meant a native New Zealander.) The prisoners threw cigarettes, biscuits — whatever they had. We didn't want to be there, but at least we were given a great welcome into the famous Stalag VIIIB!

These British chaps were tanned and, much to our surprise and relief, looked relatively healthy. Hearing of our arrival, they had given up their daily ration of cabbage soup — full of worms and sand — for us to eat. We didn't have anything to eat this soup out of; I ate mine out of my boot. Some of the others ate it off the ground. It tasted putrid, but at least it was hot and it was the only food we'd had in days. We were put into a large compound right at the end of the camp, which was known to the British as the WOG compound. As there were two latrines in the compound, we were asked by RSM Beesley of the Third Commando to use only the large latrine. The smaller one would be left for other races and nationalities — Muslims, Sikhs, Hindus, Palestinians, and Arabs — as they had objected to white Christians using the same latrine.

On the first night, a number of our chaps had borrowed musical instruments from some of the British people in the camp. There were two violin players from Manitoba, a couple of guitar players, and a banjo player. When these fellows played, they intrigued the whole camp, including the Germans, with their old time country music. It was hard to believe that this great music was being played under such hopeless conditions.

Later on, the Dieppe Canadians were moved to another compound — Block 6, located directly across from the RAF compound. During our first night in Block 6, two dogs running at large in the compound leaped through an open window (there was no glass in any of the windows). As many of the men didn't have bunks, the dogs attacked the men lying on the floor underneath the windows. The men seized the dogs and strangled them. To dispose of them, they were sent to the cook house in the *kubels* that were used to bring up the mint tea first thing that morning. The dogs were then cut up and burned in the fire boxes where the soup was cooked. The Germans hunted for the dogs for days, but never found out what happened to them. They even pumped out the latrines in their search, but to no avail.

On October 8, 1942, we were suddenly moved back to the WOG compound, where there was more room for the Germans to surround us with machine guns and armoured vehicles. The guards in the towers had been doubled. We prisoners were concerned by these developments, and wondered what was taking place. Two days later we were returned to Block 6.

We heard a long speech by a German officer, condemning us for tying the hands of German prisoners during the Dieppe raid. (This had been done to prevent the prisoners from destroying any documents they might have had, and to make it easier to control them on the boats returning to England. It became apparent that the Canadians would not be able to get these German prisoners back to England. Later, the Germans found their comrades shot with their hands still tied.)

We were marched away in tens toward one of the huts. We all believed we were going to be shot, and we were determined to die like soldiers. However, to our amazement, the Germans stood with ropes over their shoulders, calling us "*Gangster schwein.*" They told us that our hands were to be tied crosswise in front, and this would continue until Winston Churchill apologized for the tying of Germans and promised that it would never happen again. Churchill ignored this demand and decided to tie up German prisoners in England and Canada, which resulted in all the airmen in the Air Force compound also having their hands tied. A unit of crack German troops had been brought from the Russian front to patrol the huts and the latrine to make sure no one had managed to untie his hands.

Morale was at an all-time low. We would have to go to the latrine in groups of ten with a *sanitator* (the German word for stretcher bearer) to pull our pants down and up again when we were finished. There was no wiping to do as there was nothing to wipe with. This was very demoralizing. There were Gestapo searches where we stood outside in the cold for hours. To top it all off, the huts were infested with bed bugs, fleas, lice, rats, and, in the summer, millions of flies. Rats were running rampant in the latrine. One man's job was to kill rats. He would be paid one cigarette for every rat he killed. During the time our hands were tied with rope a rat leaped and grabbed a man's testicles. The man sitting on the next hole reached over — with his hands tied — and choked the rat until it let go. However, it was necessary to remove one of the man's testicles.

The first night after our hands were tied, three members of the Royal Regiment cut a hole through the wire fence behind the latrine in the WOG compound and escaped. They were Tom McClymont, Bob Wignis, and Alex Sinclair. Ten days later they were picked up and brought back and were made to stand against the wall outside with their hands chained behind their backs for a whole day. They then served ten days solitary confinement in the bunker. (Later, I was sorry to hear that one of these men, Bob Wignis, was shot and killed on another escape attempt a year after the first.)

Smiling in Germany during the war was forbidden — not just for POWs, but for German citizens as well. I was punched in the face by a German officer for smiling when my hands were being tied. This was not the only harsh punishment I received. One day I had a terrible headache and was really depressed. I put my collar up on my greatcoat and squatted down on the floor, all hunched up, with my head in my hands and my wrists tied with rope. A German guard came over yelling, "Sitting down is *verboten!*" giving me a terrific kick with his jack boot just below the ribcage, only adding to my headache. This kind of treatment was the norm.

For more than twelve months, I ate out of a tin can, using the sharp lid as a spoon. Eventually, we received a bowl and a mug that had been sent to us by the Swedish Red Cross. The Germans did not supply anything. All medical and dental supplies, blankets, clothing, and even the delouser were shipped through the Red Cross from Britain.

The winter of 1942–43 had been terrible. Our hands were tied with rope all through October and November. The huts

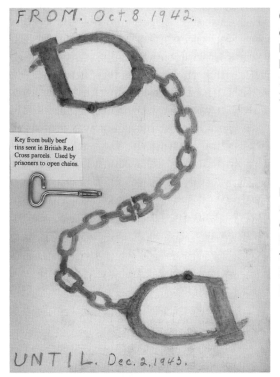

FROM. Oct. 8 1942.

Key from bully beef tins sent in British Red Cross parcels. Used by prisoners to open chains.

UNTIL. Dec. 2, 1943.

Chains similar to this one (sketched by Jack Poolton) were worn by POWs from October 8, 1942, until December 2, 1943.

Prisoners would be able to open their chains by using the keys from bully beef tins that came in British Red Cross parcels.

were unheated, with no glass in the windows — just cardboard and sacking. There were large potholes in the cement floor. Most of the men were wearing wooden clogs that were made in the camp, as many were getting chilblains from the cold going through the leather soles of their boots. The men weren't allowed to lie on their bunks during the daytime. They had to stand or else squat on the floor because there was nothing to sit on. The Germans had stopped all Red Cross parcels, cigarettes, and incoming and outgoing mail, and we were strictly on German rations — an experience that is almost impossible to forget. My mind would wander back to the swill that we fed the pigs on the family farm.

One of the hardest things we had to bear was the absence of hearing female voices speaking English. And it was extremely hard at Christmas time, missing family, food, and Christmas carols.

Early in December 1942, the Germans brought in the chains. Compared to the ropes, which contained creosote and were causing ugly sores on the men's wrists, this was a godsend as we could get our hands in our pockets for warmth. There was about fifteen inches of chain with a swivel in the middle. The chains were put on at 06:00 hours and taken off at about 20:00 hours. Altogether, we spent 410 days in ropes and chains. (Unknown to the Goons, we could unlock the chains with the little flat key used to open the bully beef tins that were in the Red Cross parcels. Woebetide the man that was caught with his chains off.)

The *block führer* for the Canadians in block six was an S.O.B. that we called Spitfire. Everybody hated the bastard. His high cheekbones gave him the appearance of a Mongolian, and he always had a snarl on his face. Whenever he was seen approaching, someone would yell "air raid" to warn us that he was coming. It was apparent that he hated Canadians with a passion and was going to make our stay at Stalag VIIIB as miserable as possible. One day I had just got a pot of water to the boil. I was down on my hands and knees on the floor using pieces of cardboard and slivers of wood for fuel and was just about to drop the tea into the pot when Spitfire came through the hut. He took a run and kicked my pot flying, scalding me in the process.

We were counted twice a day, everyday, including Christmas. It appeared the Germans could only count in fives and whenever there was a man short we might be counted as many as twenty times. I recall one occasion when there was an extra man in the count. This caused more confusion than when they were a man short.

There were loudspeakers placed around the camp. We would continually get the German news in English, from the traitor Lord "Haw Haw" William Joyce. If we believed a lot of this news we would have gone insane for they seemed to have sunk the British Navy three times over, shot down a thousand aircraft, and taken a million POWs.

Later on we would get the BBC news from London as several radios had found their way into the camp. I was able to listen to the news on a radio that was hidden inside a piano accordion in the air force compound.

Often, we would get pleasure from tormenting our captors. Early one morning the guard came in to the hut with his box of chains to begin the long procedure of "chaining up the prisoners." As each prisoner stepped forward to have his chains put on, the ones with their chains already on would sneak around his back, unlock their chains, and quickly and carefully place them back in the box. An officer arrived to ask the guard what he had been doing for four hours. His answer was that he had been chaining the prisoners.

There were times when a prisoner would have his greatcoat on one minute and off the next. This would really confuse the Germans. Spitfire, the block führer, walked through the washroom one day and observed a prisoner standing naked, washing himself, with his chains on. Spitfire barked, "How did this man remove his clothing?"

Someone retorted, "He's a magician."

Spitfire shrugged his shoulders, turned and left. Another man was caught naked with his chains on. By the time the guard rushed out and brought in an officer, the man was fully clothed. The guard was charged with being drunk on duty. (Any man that was caught with his chains off would have his hands chained behind his back and would be stood outside with his nose and toes touching the wall, regardless of the weather.)

What helped us tolerate the ropes and chains was, first of all, the knowledge that we were keeping these crack German troops away from any of the fronts, and, second, our training as soldiers.

Christmas Day, 1942 had passed. (The chains were removed for that one day: the Germans were human after all.) Now it was January 16, 1943. I had received no mail from home yet, and had been in ropes and chains for one hundred days.

February 8, 1943, I received my first letter from home — dated October 13, 1942. At least this proved that my family knew I was alive.

It was over three months before the Dieppe prisoners were allowed out of the compound for a shower, which would usually last two minutes or less. There would be twelve or fifteen men struggling to get under the shower head before it was turned off. The Germans would be pointing to the men's penises; if they spotted someone who had been circumcised they would shout "*Juden*!" meaning Jew. However, no one paid any attention to this. The Germans believed anyone that was circumcised was a Jew.

The worst crime a POW could commit was to steal from his

comrades. That first winter, a Canadian in hut 20A was caught stealing. He was severely beaten, and, as no one would defend him, he had to be moved to another hut for his own protection.

This happened while we were strictly on German rations, which consisted of a cup full of cabbage or turnip soup that at times would contain parts of the heads of animals, such as jaws with teeth, eyes with parts of the hide still attached, and, on one occasion, the skeleton of a rat. And then there was the bed board soup that contained slivers of wood, and the fish cheese that you could smell long before it reached the compound.

As I have already mentioned, the cabbage would be full of worms and sand; one could always tell when the soup was coming by the horrible smell. Later, the boiled potatoes would arrive. Usually, there would be three to a man, but one of the three would always be rotten. About mid-afternoon, the black bread would arrive. As we would mostly be in groups of eight with a selected group leader, it was his job to cut the loaf into equal pieces. We would all draw a number that would be under the pieces, so that everything was done fairly.

There might be a small portion of margarine or synthetic jam; this, however, would be given out by groups, then divided among the members of the group. In the end you might only get margarine or jam every three or four months.

Other than the mint tea, which we would use for shaving, that would be the day's ration. It is not surprising that someone might be tempted to steal.

Our packages from home often contained cigarettes. Prior to the Canadians arriving at Stalag VIIIB, parcels containing cigarettes would all be dumped out of the packages and broken in half in case they contained maps or messages. By the time cigarettes started to arrive from Canada, the breaking in half had ceased, but they were still all dumped out of the packages. Eventually we received them in the cartons.

Three of four times a year, the Germans would read us the "riot act," which turned into quite a joke. It always started out with "Any prisoner striking a German officer will be court-martialled, and if found guilty, will be shot! Any prisoner, failing to salute a German officer, will face imprisonment! Any prisoner, striking a German soldier will be court-martialled, and if found guilty, will face imprisonment! Any prisoner caught with a German woman will face imprisonment! Any prisoner caught having sexual intercourse with a German woman will be shot! All foreign women in Germany are entitled to the same protection and privileges as German women!" As each commandment was read out, a great cheer would be heard from a thousand or more prisoners.

At times I would look up at the moon on a clear night and try to picture the same moon shining over the farm back home.

Ten
The Tunnel

Sometime in March 1943, while the chains were on, it was decided that a tunnel would be dug from the Dieppe compound. A sergeant major went from hut to hut telling everybody about it. He said that as long as everybody knew about it, nobody would need to talk about it. The tunnel was dug and completed under adverse conditions: the men's hands were in chains, and crack German troops were patrolling the huts, yard, and latrine. Completing this huge task was just short of a miracle. It was ingenious. When the tunnel was discovered, owing to the first snow that fell the fall of 1943, a German general remarked that it was a pity that men who could complete such a task under the noses of their German captors were not allies, but enemies.

Early in March 1943, we were all told that a tunnel was to be dug in the Dieppe Compound and that everyone would participate. This news really raised our morale. The tunnel was finished by May and people were going through, both in daylight and at night. We knew that security was vital and that with everyone knowing that a tunnel was being dug, there would be no reason to talk about it.

The tunnel was in hut 19B, as it was closest to the main fence, which had double-barbed wire about ten feet apart. This space between the wire was filled with concertina wire, tin cans hanging with stones inside that would rattle if anyone was trying to get through or trying to cut the wire. The tunnel would have to go under two roads: one inside the fence that would carry teams and wagons, and one outside the fence that marching German troops, trucks, and tanks travelled on.

A hole had to be cut in the concrete floor beneath one of the bunks. This had to be in the form of a slab that could be replaced when the tunnel had to be sealed in the event of a Gestapo search. A shaft was sunk to a depth of approximately ten feet. The tunnel was at least 140 feet long. It would come up just short of the pine trees they had aimed for, and to the right and just behind the goon tower. When the tunnel was completed it had electric lights, and a type of track with a trolley, fashioned from Red Cross food tins, that was used first to pull the dirt back to the shaft during digging, and later when escapees were going through, lying on their bellies on the trolley. A long pipe had been fashioned from klim tins joined together and reached the full length of the tunnel. These were in the Canadian Red Cross parcels and contained milk powder. A bellows was made from a kit bag and someone would keep working this to pump air to the end of the tunnel where the digging was going on. Mostly, the men would work in their underwear, but some preferred to work in the nude. It was very hard to get the sand off the clothing, and if the Germans happened to see sand on anyone it would be a dead giveaway.

We had to be very careful. I did not do any of the digging on this tunnel, but helped dig tunnels while on working parties. However, I helped to make the tool that was used to do most of the digging, which was done mainly by Canadian engineers. I also helped, along with many others, to distribute the sand as it was brought to the surface.

The escape committee gave priority to those who spoke a second language and would supply them with forged papers, work permits, etc.; clothing made from blankets; and dyed uniforms, fedora hats, and brief cases. These prisoners had the highest likelihood of success. All these items were made in the camp, unknown to the Germans. Whenever several men were prepared to go out someone would have to cut the wire fence in one of the other compounds and make it look like the escapees had gone from there. This was to keep suspicion away from the Dieppe compound. They would have the dogs outside the fence trying to pick up the trail that was not there. As we were counted twice each day, the count in the Canadian compound had to be correct. People were brought in from other compounds to do this.

Some of the people leaving through the tunnel had information that would be very important to the allied war effort — if they were lucky enough to make it back. I could have gone through the tunnel at night in battle dress, but with no help such as papers and other such items, I would have had a limited chance of success and may have jeopardized the tunnel.

I recall an escape attempt one afternoon in which several men came up out of the ground and walked quietly into the pine trees just behind the goon tower. The German guard in the tower was distracted by one of our men, who engaged the guard in a heated argument to divert his attention from the escape.

The material from the tunnel was used to make flower beds between the huts. Sand was carried down the men's pant legs and gradually shaken out as they would move around. It had to be mixed in with the soil that was already there. The beds were getting higher by the day up to the height of twelve inches or more. The block führer known as "Spitfire" would come by and ask when we were going to plant the seeds. As far as I know there were never any seeds. There would be men with rakes continually raking to mix the sand in so that it would not be so noticeable.

At times the German troops marching on the road outside were told to goose-step as they marched past the camp in order to intimidate those of us on the inside. This could have been dangerous for the tunnel as the ground would literally tremble as they marched across it. They were also ordered to sing one of their songs of hate. However, this did not affect us and we would applaud them. To support the tunnel where it went under the outside road — and under goose-stepping German troops — a new flagpole the Germans were preparing was stolen, cut up, and used in the tunnel for supports.

While the tunnel was being dug, a German contractor was brought in to the camp to build reservoirs in case of fire. For propaganda purposes, these reservoirs were presented as swimming pools. However, they were fenced in and no one ever had the opportunity to swim in them. The reservoirs ended up being used for another purpose: one morning, a man was found drowned. The Germans made an announcement that everyone should go down and try to identify this man — which no one could do. Apparently, he was a German spy who had been discovered and deliberately drowned.

On arrival, the contractor was approached by several of the prisoners, volunteering to help with the work on the condition that they were paid in cement. The contractor was taken through the huts and shown the huge potholes in the cement floor. The cement, he was told, would be used to patch up these holes. However, the cement was used in the tunnel and the potholes were never repaired.

At least fifty men left through the tunnel. Several of them were South African officers, all of whom could speak German. They had managed somehow to get in to Stalag VIIIB for the purpose of escaping. I don't know if any of them ever made it to freedom.

Eventually, when snow fell, heat from the tunnel melted the snow on the hatch, leaving a square shape, and the Germans discovered the tunnel. Shortly afterwards, another tunnel was started in hut 20B.

Eleven

Escape

Jack constantly had escape on his mind, and since the failed attempt on the train, it had intensified. He was so desperate that he decided to try it alone. He still remembered what the Germans said when they first captured the Canadians — "Für euch ist der krieg zu ende (For you the war is over)" — and he wanted to prove them wrong. Jack believed escaping was food for the conscience.

Throughout the winter I had been planning to make a break. I would go to sleep and wake up in the morning thinking and planning. I would try to brainwash myself into believing that I could successfully escape and make it back to my regiment in England. When I approached the escape committee about going through the tunnel, I was asked by my regimental sergeant major, Guy Murray of the Royal Regiment of Canada, how many languages I could speak. I answered, "One, sir. English."

He informed me that they could not give me any help such as papers, civilian clothes, etc. when I could not speak another language. However, he gave me a compass telling me never to reveal where it came from. As I had not found anyone in the Dieppe compound to go with me, I decided to go alone. I said that I was going to find a change-over, go out, and escape from a work party.

(While the ropes and chains were on, Dieppe and air force POWs were not allowed out of the camp or even near the main gate, as we were being punished. This is why a change-over was necessary. A "change-over" was someone who was assigned to a work party who you could switch identities with. The change-over would be a prisoner who did not want to go out on a work party, and who would therefore be willing to switch identities with someone who wanted to make an escape attempt.)

As I left RSM Guy Murray, he said, "Poolton, good luck. Hope you make it. Be careful and don't sell your life cheap." These words rang in my ears long after we parted.

Later that day I borrowed a Red Cross arm band from a *sanitator*, left the compound through the guarded gate, and headed for the working compound on the far side of the camp, down near the main gate. There I found George Jones, a Dunkirk POW of the British Gloucestershire Regiment who was about to be sent out to a brick factory and did not want to go. He readily agreed to accept my proposal that I go out in his place. I would have to memorize his regimental number, his POW number, where and when he was captured, etc. I still remember that POW number to this day: 10153. We would exchange Stalag identity disks and he would go to the Dieppe compound wearing the Red Cross armband, take my place, and wear my chains while I was away. This was one of the many things you had to do to make an escape attempt. It was very dangerous business. Three members of my regiment were shot and killed while escaping in Germany.

The working compound was made up of a mixed bunch: Australians, New Zealanders, South Africans, British, and, unbeknown to me at the time, three change-over airmen: two British and one Canadian. The next day the Germans came to pick up five men for the brick factory at Patschkau. This was known as an *Arbeits Kommando* (working party). Before leaving the Stalag you were searched and checked for mug shots. Your kit was gone through to the extent that a bayonet was plunged into any Red Cross food tins. I had put the compass, which was about the size of a beer cap but twice as thick on its side, in a small tin of English margarine. As the bayonet more or less hit dead centre, it missed the compass, so I had succeeded in getting it through the search. Three of the men seemed to be together and the fifth was on his own. I passed inspection without too much trouble. The three men together also got through but the fifth man, George, had all kinds of problems. They checked, re-checked, checked again, and eventually brought out his fingerprints before finally clearing him. The funny thing was that he was the only one that wasn't a change-over.

We were marched to the railway station at Lamsdorf and put into a cattle truck (the same type used to transport the Jews to the death camps). The truck we were in had been used for coal. We were locked in and had to sit in the coal dust. Eventually, we arrived at Patschkau and were marched to the brick factory. The owner of the brick factory was a Nazi type named Kuntz. He loathed the British, who had called him "Busty," owing to his potbelly.

The men were all from British regiments taken prisoner at Dunkirk. They made us welcome, but had their doubts about whether I was a member of the Gloucestershire Regiment. They were very suspicious and tripped me up on questions.

Later that evening I observed two of the group of three working on a compass. I approached them and said, "I have one of those. Are you out here to make a break?" They told me that they were and that they were airmen who had changed over. I mentioned that I was here for the same reason and that we should join forces. They agreed and accepted me. From then on we were a foursome. This was a break for me as one of the airmen could speak, read, and write German.

The next day it was off to work. I was sent out to the pits where the blue clay had to be shovelled onto a conveyor that took it into the factory. The leader of the work party was there to show me what to do. We got talking and he said to me, "Come clean. Who the hell are you and who are those other three blokes?"

The Germans were known to put spies in among the prisoners to gather information, and knowing that sooner or later we would have to tell them, I said I was a Dieppe Canadian, I had changed over with Jones, and the other three were airmen and we were all out here to make a break. I asked him if there was anyone who could not be trusted. He almost bear-hugged me. He wanted news of England and the war. He grabbed and shook my hand. Being the first Canadian soldier these chaps had ever met, I became very popular and over the next few weeks made many friends. I know I left them with a good impression of a Canadian soldier.

In the brick factory while working with a particular machine, I deliberately pushed a shovel into a rotating auger and stalled the machine. It had to be rotated backwards in order to get the shovel out. This would usually mean about three hours of down time. I did the same thing on two other occasions, and was warned. My excuse was that I had never worked around machinery before. They promptly moved me from this job and I was sent to work in the ovens where one could not do much damage. There the heat and dryness would take all of the moisture out of the skin. While working in the ovens, an English chap and myself stopped Busty from kicking two Polish slave girls to death for accidentally upsetting a trolley of green bricks they were bringing to the ovens.

I felt terrible about the women being punished, as I had caused the spill by running out of the oven and setting the switch half open on the miniature railway track where it turned to go into the oven. The girls could not see this as they were pushing the trolley from behind.

Most of the prisoners worked stripped to the waist. I had "Canada" tattooed on both upper arms, for which I was questioned several times by the Germans. As I had changed over with an Englishman, this was causing a bit of confusion. *"Englander oder Kanadisch?"*

I explained that when King George VI and Queen Elizabeth had visited Canada in 1939, I had been one of the escorts that went with them and I liked Canada so much that I had Canada tattooed on both arms. They accepted this. A German woman, a supervisor who smelled of sauerkraut, insisted on pawing me and looking at my tattoos. I asked Gilmour, who spoke German, to tell her to keep her filthy hands to herself.

We worked there for three weeks doing all the damage we could, which included all the bricks that we helped to make during the time we were there. The green bricks were taken out to the racks to dry before going to the ovens. We made sure that one of the four of us was the last person to handle them. The bricks would be passed in twos from hand to hand to be placed in the racks, at which point we would slap them together and crack them in the centre, rendering them useless.

The room that we slept in was of stone and cement with very thick walls, and two windows with bars. Earlier, I had sampled the material around the bars by chipping. The Germans had noticed it and patched it up. This was very alarming, and told us they were on the alert.

I had picked up a screwdriver with a steel handle in the factory. This is the tool we would use to get the bars out. Meantime, some Poles in the factory had given us two good maps, showing rivers and railroads.

One of the airmen, Ian Gilmour, and I used to put on boxing gloves. I would also spar with Percy "Tiger" Stubbs of the Royal Navy. He was fifty-one years old, but at one time had held a championship in the navy. He would come roaring at me with his head down and his arms flailing, and I would hit him with an uppercut. The Germans would come from miles around to watch us spar. It didn't take much to amuse them. They called me Walter Neusel after a former German boxer.

On Saturday night, we decided to make our escape, having worked until 13:00 hours that day. The Germans had a bit of a makeshift shower in the factory. We were having a final shower when two Polish girls dashed in with two round loaves of black bread tucked in the elastic band of their underpants beneath their dresses. They whipped them out, passed them to us, and bolted, hoping not to be seen by the Germans as this was an unforgivable crime. After the shower, I slipped unseen back into the factory and cut the drive belt on the steam engine.

That night at about 21:00 hours, I began to work on the window. Before getting to the bars, I had to rip out a glass window that was on the inside. (There were two glass windows that opened inward from the centre, and latched on a jamb that went up and down in the middle. I took out the right-hand window.)

Next I attacked the bars with the screwdriver, using a stove grate as a hammer. The bars were in a grid pattern: the two horizontal bars went into the wall about six inches, while the two vertical bars were cut off flush at the top and bottom. The bars were welded together where they crossed. I tried to chip into the cement where the bars went into the walls so that we could pull the bars out.

The boys had an old wind-up gramophone that they had scrounged with one record in Italian, "O Sole Mio." They played this over and over again to deaden the sound as the Germans were in the next room. I went into a frenzy with the chipping as now there was no turning back, while the other three lads stood there, saying, "Let me have a go. Let me have a go." But I wanted to finish the job myself: these boys had taken me into their group, and I felt like I owed it to them to do this job.

Eventually I chipped away enough cement so that we would be able to pull the bars towards us and bend them out of their holes, but we found that we could only pull the bars so far before the hard wood jamb stopped us. The only way we could remove the bars was to cut out the jamb, which I attempted with a small pen knife. This turned out to be the hardest part of the job, as the jamb was made of a very hard wood. I chipped away around the bottom of the jamb, making notches and narrowing the jamb like a beaver would nibble away on a tree. When I figured that I had cut the jamb enough that we could break it, we wrapped a tunic around the top to deaden the sound, and I gave one reef on it and it snapped. I reached in, grabbed the bars, and handed them to the nearest man and proceeded to knock the barbed wire off that was stapled criss-cross on the outside. With this done we had the open window before us.

It was raining lightly. The palm of my right hand was raw and bleeding. Within moments the airmen were going. I was the last man to leave and as I left I was being wished good luck and shaking hands, which made me feel good. It was kind of like leaving family — except we had ruined their work party. I went through the window with the tune "O Sole Mio" ringing in my ears.

Outside, we had to climb a twelve-foot brick wall that had glass embedded on the top with a paved road on the other side that was patrolled by a sentry. By the time I got to the wall, Ian Gilmour was on top laying on his stomach on the glass, bringing the other people up over the top of him. We had to drop down the other side, crouch at the bottom of the wall with faces turned away, and, at the same time, remove boots. (Our boots, being steel shod, would be too noisy when crossing the road.) Then we would have to wait until the sentry was far enough away. This was all done at intervals. We had to cross a man-made canal with very steep banks and about three feet of water in the bottom. In order to do this, we removed our socks, rolled up our pant legs, and went down and up the other side where we replaced our socks and boots and headed due south for Yugoslavia. The airmen were hoping that we could contact the Partisans and they would aid us in being repatriated back to England.

We travelled all night in the rain. When we came to a creek or stream we would try to throw the dogs off by walking for some distance in the water and then walking in the opposite direction when we came to another creek. Periodically, we would stop and check the compasses to make sure we were still heading south. By dawn it had stopped raining. We had reached the foothills of the Sudaten Mountains, which were part of the Carpathians. Walking down a bush road, we were alarmed to hear German voices, and just had time to dive to one side where there was a bit of a rise with shrubs growing on it. We got down in a squat and turned our faces away just as three German soldiers came around a bend with girls on their arms. They passed within a few yards of us, but did not see us as we were all wearing army battle dress, with no spats, no insignias, and no hats; the uniform effectively allowed us to blend into the landscape. We continued on toward the mountains, which were covered with timber. We had to be on the lookout for wolves and wild boar.

Being raised in Northern Ontario on a farm, I was very familiar with the bush. It was my job to lead the way whenever we were travelling through bush — which we could do by day to keep ourselves hidden — while the airmen took over at night when we were travelling by the stars.

It was very exhausting climbing to the top of the mountain, where we could look down on a beautiful green valley knowing that we had to go down and up again. I can't remember how many times we did this. While crossing the mountains, we were stopped twice by what was known as an *ober-fester*. *Ober-festers* were in charge of the forests and had the authority to shoot anyone. They carried double-barreled shotguns, wore green uniforms and green hats with feathers in them, and looked like Robin Hood. On one occasion, we said we were working in the area. The *ober-fester* didn't believe us, so we just kept walking, not looking back. The man was screaming for us to halt as we went around a bend and out of range. We also had to detour around workmen that were cutting timber.

Eventually, we got through the mountains and into the flat farmlands of Czechoslovakia. We had crossed the mountains by daylight, and now we would have to travel at night and lay up in the daytime. There were mostly wheat fields, which was a good thing because any food we had left with was gone. We would now survive from wheat by filling our pockets with the heads and eating them when stopping to rest. I could not believe there were no turnips, cabbage, or carrots, and the potatoes were the size of marbles this time of the year (late July and early August). One night raiding a garden, the Canadian airman jumped the fence and started to throw out heads of lettuce. I said to him, "Throw out something else!" He said, "There is nothing else." Another night we were held up by a scarecrow in a potato patch. It looked so real I had to roll out into the middle of the patch to look at it from a different angle to realize what it was. At the same time, several dogs started barking so we got out of there fast. Adding to our difficulties was the fact that it was haying season, which meant that the farmers were out at 05:00 hours and up until 21:00. This cut down our travelling time. As well, there was a curfew.

We slept in coils of hay on several occasions. One time I happened to hear the wagon coming down the field with farmers taking in the hay. We had to make a break for cover when the farmers were only two coils away from me. A woman with several kids threatened us with a scythe that she was using and screamed obscenities when we gave her the finger. I don't believe she knew who we were.

Getting bolder — something we had been warned against — we would walk through villages and towns at night, taking shortcuts. Several times we'd pass German soldiers coming out of pubs. The one airman would tie a white handkerchief around his arm and yell "*heil Hitler*" and say goodnight in German and just keep walking. As everyone h*eil*ed Hitler, they would *heil* Hitler back. We would have to break step so that we didn't look too military, as we might get picked up as German deserters.

We were heading for a railway line, which was shown on our maps, that would take us down through Hungary. I recall that on one rainy day we spent the afternoon in some bushes near a town observing a guarded railway bridge (not on the line we were seeking). The guard was on the far side where he had a sentry box. We first attempted to jump a moving train, but this turned out to be very dangerous and almost impossible, and if two got on and the others did not, they would have to jump off again, as we did not want to be separated. That evening after dark we crossed at intervals, carrying our boots, and dropped down on the other side without being seen.

We were carrying twenty-eight bars of English Red Cross soap, hoping to barter it for food, information, or whatever we needed. Up until this time we had not tried to contact anyone:

there was no way of knowing who to trust. If we approached the wrong person, it would mean being handed over to the Gestapo. We had to keep in mind that there was a bounty on escaped prisoners of war, and we would be running a risk of being sold out if we didn't watch who we dealt with. We decided to wait until we had reached Hungary and try there.

I still did not know the proper names of my three companions, and to them I was known only as Jonesy.

As we travelled, the airmen would talk about stealing a German aircraft, which would have to already be fueled up and able to carry four men. They would try to fly the plane to Turkey. We did not know at that time that the Allies had landed in Sicily. This good news would surely have raised our hopes, and would have provided us with a more promising destination. I was thankful in a way that the airmen could not find a German aircraft, as I had never been in a plane before.

When we began the journey we had agreed that if one of us was ever stopped the other three would bolt, if possible. When we made this agreement we never expected that it would come into play as soon as it did.

One morning at about 04:30, while looking for a place to rest up and spend the daylight hours, we came across an outpost that looked abandoned. Suddenly, however, out of nowhere appeared a German soldier. He shoved a rifle into my navel and shouted "halt!" The airmen bolted through a wheat field in a crouch trying to keep their heads down and out of sight. The German was yelling "halt" out of the corner of his mouth, at the same time keeping his eyes on me. I stood there alone, my hands shoulder high, palms exposed, while he kept saying "*pistoli*," "*pistoli*," meaning did I have a pistol. He was shaking and appeared very nervous. My eyes were moving from his eyes to his finger on the trigger. I thought he might pull the trigger by accident. The thought of disarming him was going through my mind as we had been trained to do this, but if I failed, it would mean a bullet in the guts. The German had at least three female companions and while one was on the phone, another attempted to frisk me. They checked the kit bag and discovered the twenty-eight bars of soap, which they dumped on the ground and counted. I had to smile to myself hearing them counting the bars in unison: "*Ein, Swei, Drei....*" They counted them back into the bag and out again, all the time smelling their fingers. I found this all very amusing.

Within minutes, three men on bicycles arrived — the Gestapo, a civilian policeman, and a German army sergeant. They put their bikes down and strutted around like three roosters. The Gestapo walked up to me, his face almost touching mine and asked, "*Franzose?*", wanting to know if I was French.

I replied in German, "*Nein, Englander.*"

They all repeated "*Englander*" in unison and pulled out their pistols. The Gestapo put his pistol on the end of my nose and pressed on it. I could see that the barrel was rusty, another thing I found very comical. Several thoughts were going through my mind: I worried that they would find the compass, as I had sworn never to reveal where it had come from; I knew that, if I were shot, my family would never know what happened to me as I was carrying another man's identification; and I remembered the remarks made by RSM Guy Murray back at Stalag VIIIB when he told me not to sell my life cheap.

The Germans took my belt and braces, and I had to hold my pants up by hand. The Gestapo asked for my tunic so they could search it. The compass was in the left inside pocket. I removed the tunic, and as I passed it around in front of me I slipped my right hand into the pocket, grabbed the compass, changed hands, and handed him the tunic with the compass in my right hand. They checked all the pockets and handed it back. I put the tunic back on with the compass still in my hand. They led me over to where they had found three tracks. As I had already told them that I had only one comrade with me, the Gestapo became enraged. He called me an English swine and struck me on the nose with his fist. Blood flew and I saw stars. I was still holding my pants up, and, luckily was able to drop the compass and put my foot on it. This pushed it into the soft earth. It was a great relief to be rid of it. They gave me my belt and braces back, as well as the kit bag with the soap. There was much talking in German that I couldn't understand, but I knew it was referring to me.

Finally, the Gestapo pointed with his arm and said, "up march," which meant march off, down a road. It was starting to get light. He marched me about three or four kilometres towards a farm and stayed about ten feet behind me the entire way. I thought he might shoot me in the back, and I was wondering what it was going to feel like.

With my nose still bleeding, we arrived at the farm. The

Gestapo woke the farmer, who was also the jailer. There was a cell that was part of the barn and, as it was haying season, they had piled hay in front of the door. The farmer got an old woman out to move the hay. She then opened the door, went inside, and dragged an old straw-filled mattress out, leaving me with just the bare boards. They pushed me in and locked the door.

I don't think anyone had been in this cell for at least eighty or ninety years. It was damp, and had mould on the walls and insects of all types. There was a small window with bars. I immediately checked them to see if I could get the bars out. As I had no tool of any kind to work with, it was impossible.

The next day they brought a German who could speak English in to interview me. The entire time he was in the cell, the jailer stood there with his pistol pointed at me. The English-speaking German asked me where I was from and who I was. Of course, I told him a bunch of lies and gave him a sermon on the Geneva convention. I told him that a British soldier was not supposed to be held in a civilian jail. Then he politely told me, "You are lucky that you were not shot." Before he left, I demanded that I be returned to Stalag VIIIB immediately, as I was in danger being in this civilian jail cell.

During the four days and nights I was held in this cell, I was given boiled potato peelings twice, but never any water. At least the potato peelings were hot. I had to eat them with my fingers reaching through the bars, as the pot they were in was too big to be pushed through. The kids would come and throw stones through the window, which had no glass, and would scream "*schwein hund*," meaning pig dog. They would also spit. When I look back on this, I find it hard to believe that it actually happened to me. If it hadn't been for our vigorous training, discipline, and determination to escape, I don't think I could have endured any of this, particularly the isolation and loneliness.

I passed my time in the cell looking out my window. I would often see civilians going down to the river to wash. It seemed that they did not have any shoes. Watching the geese by the river also kept me amused.

Early on the morning of the fifth day, a cocky young guard arrived to take me back to Stalag VIIIB. When the cell door was opened, even with the guard present, the old jailer still had his pistol in his hand.

The journey back to VIIIB required two bus rides. On one there were German soldiers. While standing on the bus I brushed against a German woman dressed in black. She pulled back and started brushing her shoulder where I had touched her. The German soldiers looked at me and smiled.

We arrived at a railway station, where I was reunited with the three airmen. They had reached the main railway, and tried several times to jump a moving freight train and failed. The men were eventually rounded up by Hitler youth and dogs, men with pitch forks, and women with butcher knives and meat cleavers. All had been on the lookout for escaped POWs reported to be in the area.

At the station we asked the guard to take us to the washroom. He said it was forbidden. As we were still carrying a tin of Yardley's Lavender Brilliantine hair gel that my mother had sent me, we shoved it under his nose and told him to smell it, and if he took us to the washroom, he could have it. He accepted.

I vividly remember a Pole sitting on the station platform, his hands and ankles in chains. As the airmen still had some cigarettes, Gilmour offered a cigarette to the Pole, put it in his mouth, and lit it. A German guard came rushing over screaming, "*Verboten!*" An argument started between Gilmour and the German. Gilmour said they were his cigarettes and he would do whatever he pleased with them. He took three or more out of his package and tucked them into the Pole's jacket pocket, saying in German, "*Nix verboten*" (not forbidden).

It would have been impossible to escape from this station as it was swarming with German soldiers. We took the train back to Lamsdorf. This time we rode with the train crew, most of them women. One seemed sympathetic to the fact that we were prisoners of war, and airmen in particular. The guard continually combed his hair and smelled his fingers all the way back.

On arrival at VIIIB, we were strip-searched outside the camp to the extent that the soles of our boots were examined before we were finally allowed back in through the gates. As escaping prisoners being brought back in, we were brought up on a charge before the camp commandant. Owing to identification problems, Jones would have to go in and receive the sentence and I would have to serve it. This all had to be done unknown to the Germans, otherwise the sentence would be doubled. The fact that there was a waiting period until a cell was available in the bunker gave us time to organize this switch-over.

I was sentenced to twenty-eight days solitary confinement. It's a wonder I kept my sanity throughout this ordeal. The cell was approximately six feet by six feet with a wooden bunk about two feet wide and a foot off the floor. A bucket in the corner served as a latrine. The door was steel with a peep hole that had a shutter on the outside. It was hard to know when you were being watched. Every morning I was made to get a bucket of water and scrub the floor. The window was barred and very high. I was allowed out once a day with the other men in solitary for exercise. We were forced to walk around in circles, staying four feet apart. This was the only time we could see fellow inmates. However, we were not allowed to communicate. At times when using the latrine, we could exchange a few words, providing we were not caught.

I was fed bread and water and a cup of soup every third day. I killed flies to break the monotony. The guards were brutal. The window was up high and by jumping up and grabbing the bars I could look out into the next compound. This was where they trained the Doberman pinschers and German shepherds. They would have a dummy dressed in British battle dress with a piece of meat tied to the throat. The dogs would leap at the piece of meat.

The days in solitary were god awful compared to being in the main camp. While in the bunker, I picked up an old pocketbook. The principal figure was a gunman named Silent Sutton. As I read this book several times, I began to imagine that I was Silent Sutton, the gunslinger. I served the twenty-eight days, and returned to the Dieppe compound to take my identity back.

The escape cost me two of my mother's comfort parcels from home. She was allowed to send one every three months while I was away, and two of them had come together. George Jones used up all the items in the packages, things like articles of clothing, food, and personal items. My younger brother Victor had stopped using sugar so that it could be sent to me. Several cartons of cigarettes had also arrived, sent by other people, and George Jones had used them up. There wasn't one cigarette left for me. I didn't mind the cigarettes, but the personal things I thought he should have saved. This was part of the price I paid to make an escape attempt. Of the four escape attempts I made while a *kriegsgefangener* (POW) in Germany, this had been the most rewarding.

81

Many acts of sabotage were committed by men who were prisoners of war in Germany during World War II. If caught, and if the act had been serious enough, the punishment could have been death by firing squad. In any case, one would be severely punished. This could mean being sent to what was known as an *arbeits lager* (work camp.) These places were known as the camps of no return. No one ever came back. They would be beaten, starved, or worked to death, whichever came first.

I learned all about these camps when I was serving solitary confinement in the bunker for escaping in 1943. The cell across from mine contained a New Zealand airman, who I believe was named Larsen. He was a big man over six feet tall and had one arm in a plaster cast. As he spoke German, he acted as my interpreter when the occasion arose. Whenever we were able to exchange a few words, he told me that he had committed a very serious act of sabotage, and had been sentenced to a life of hard labour at one of these camps. He almost received the death penalty. Apparently he had thrown a steel chain into a machine at a paper factory and had done 100 million marks worth of damage. This machine could not be repaired while the war was on. He had also been a change-over at the time, out on a working party under another man's name to make an escape attempt. To try to prevent him from being sent away, the British doctors at Stalag VIIIB had broken his arm and put it in a plaster cast. This man would continually belittle the German guards at the bunker. There were also three other British prisoners in the bunker with casts on one arm. I was told that, as the bone would start to heal, the doctors would re-break it and put a new cast on, trying to delay as long as possible these men being moved out of the Stalag in the hope that the war would come to an end before the men could be moved.

After serving the first three weeks, I became very ill with pains in my stomach. While hunched over sitting on the bunk, a German guard rushed in and kicked me in the stomach. He told me it was forbidden to sit on the bunk in the daylight hours, so I sat on the floor.

One Sunday morning, the pains got worse. I was doubled over. The only people who were allowed into the bunker were the padres. This particular Sunday morning the cell doors were flung open and an Australian padre entered my cell. He put his hand on my shoulder and said, "Son, you need medical attention. I will go and speak with the doctors."

I said, "No. I've got another week to go. I can put up with it. I want to finish my sentence."

However, he left and returned with a medical officer, a New Zealand major, who said, "I am taking you out. You could die in here."

We left the cell and walked down the hallway, which was barred by two German guards with bayonets. The New Zealand major pushed the two bayonets aside and the three of us passed through. I will always remember this act of bravery and the admiration I had for this man.

They took me across the road to the *revier* (sick bay). As it was forbidden that anyone should be removed from the bunker, the German *stabsarzt* (medical corps captain) had to be contacted immediately. I sat on a chair with several British doctors standing around waiting for the German to come. When he finally appeared, the major said to me, "For Christ's sake, look sick!"

Barely looking at me, the German *stabsarzt* agreed that I was too sick to be in solitary confinement, and I would remain in the *revier* under the care of the British doctors. I was told that I had an ulcer and the best they could do for me was to feed me oatmeal in preference to cabbage or turnip soup. Being that I was an escapee and from the bunker, I got special treatment from these doctors. However, later on, when the German *stabsarzt* thought I was well enough, I was seized by two German guards and rushed back to the same cell, my feet barely touching the ground. The doctors apologized for not being able to keep me there longer. I thanked them and told them not to worry as I knew I had to go back and finish my sentence eventually.

After the escape attempt and serving the solitary confinement in the bunker, it felt good to be back in 21A of the Dieppe compound. I settled down to spending another winter wearing chains and suffering from the cold. At least we were getting Red Cross parcels fairly regularly now.

Ian Gilmour had already approached me about having another go. I told him that there was a way out of the camp. He looked surprised as I asked him to come with me to the Dieppe compound. We contacted RSM Guy Murray, and informed him that we had just made an escape attempt and wanted to know if we could go out through the tunnel. He told us that the tunnel was sealed up due to a Gestapo scare. I told him my friend could speak, read, and write German. He said that they would give him any help they could, but that I would spoil his chances of making a successful escape, not being able to speak another language. Ian could not believe that after what we had gone through together I had never once mentioned that I knew there was a tunnel in the Dieppe compound. As I had been sworn to secrecy, I didn't think it was right for me to reveal it. (Although we did not go through the tunnel we did make another attempt in the summer of 1944 from a place called Peiskretscham, not far from Hindenburg.)

Now that I was back in camp again, I learned some of the consequences of my escape attempt. It seems that when it was discovered that four prisoners had escaped from the brick factory at Patschkau, all hell broke loose. The guards were all sent to the Russian Front, and the remaining prisoners were made to work harder and longer and had their rations cut. This was always the end result of an escape.

Twelve
Foiled by the Snow

Towards the end of the chain-up, sets of chains would go missing. The Germans would make the prisoners stand outside for hours until the missing chains turned up. To try to solve this problem, the Germans began attaching prisoners' Stalag numbers to their chains so they could tell whose chains were missing.

In November 1943, a German guard brought me a note from my buddy B.L. "Red" Perry. I had not seen Perry since prior to the chain-up, when the Germans called out two working parties from the Dieppe compound. (Perry, Mawbey, and several others were sent to work in a sugar beet factory. Later on they were moved to the bush job at Poppelau, Poland.)
Perry's note said:

> Jack,
>
> I'm on a working party in the bush with a few of your chums. We're cutting trees … it's not war work. Why not give yourself a break and join us.
>
> Red.

This meant volunteering to work for the Germans, which I was strictly against. As well, this also meant another cattle-truck ride that would last for hours. However, I thought it over and realized this might be another opportunity to escape, so I accepted. This meant that I had to get another compass from the escape committee. RSM Murray gave me the compass and again wished me good luck. This compass was bigger than the first. To conceal it, I rolled it in a ball of wool taken from a scarf my mother had sent me. It survived several searches by the Gestapo. As well, I carried it with me on the death march that was to come later. I've had the compass ever since.

I joined *Arbeits Kommando* #164 a few days later. The work party was at Poppelau in Poland. Here the prisoners were cutting trees by selection. The German *meister* would blaze the trees that were to be cut, mostly pine. We would also blaze other trees that were nearby and cut them down.

We worked *drei man zusammen* (three men together). I was on the two-man saw with Perry. Mawbey would carry and pile the logs, which were a metre long. Perry knew that I was experienced with a crosscut saw, whereas most of the other men were not. I believe that was another reason why he sent me the note. It made the work much harder with someone who was inexperienced, as there was a quota that we had to meet before returning to camp.

We had at least a three-kilometre walk to the job. On the way

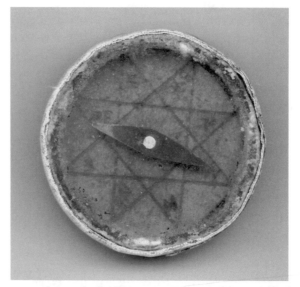

This compass was made by the escape committee at Stalag VIIIB. It was entrusted to Jack by RSM Guy Murray of the Royal Regiment for an escape attempt.

back, we carried as many branches as we were allowed to pick up to be used as firewood. A fire was necessary on the job as our feet were always soaking wet, owing to the leather army boots, which were not waterproof.

Jim Mawbey had somehow gotten involved repairing the fire boxes of the *kessels* (kettles) where they cooked the soup. He had convinced the Germans that these fireboxes periodically needed to be repaired, and that he had been an expert on this type of job. If they would agree, he would stay in Saturday mornings instead of going to the bush and do the necessary repairs on the fireboxes. This went on for months. With Christmas fast approaching, Jim convinced the Germans that the fireboxes were in such bad shape they could break down over Christmas and that he needed an extra man to assist him the Saturday before Christmas. I was chosen to accompany him. The night before, Jim explained to me that we would be searching to find the one particular type of clay that would fix the fireboxes, but cautioned, "We must have the guard Peter because if we get that S.O.B. Erik, things might not work out the way I have planned."

At this time I did not know what he was talking about. Saturday morning arrived, and to our astonishment there stood Erik waiting to take us out!

The three of us started out. Jim had the shovel and I had the pail. Jim dug three or four clay samples, walking in the direction of the village of Poppelau, and each time declared, "This is not the right type of clay, move on."

We kept going until we arrived at the village. Jim happened to find the proper clay, right beside the *backerei* (bakery), which, of course, was all part of his plan. Jim had been doing the same routine with the other guard, Peter, for weeks. But Erik had never been on this mission before. We were not sure how he would react. Jim dropped his shovel and told me to drop the pail and follow him. In the meantime, he was stuffing a handful of cigarettes into Erik's pocket.

We entered the *backerei*. Jim handed me three loaves of white bread, which I stuffed in my tunic. He grabbed a knife and sliced through a type of cake called *kuchen*, folded it up and then turned around to where there was a bag of *mehl* (flour), and filled his hat. We then headed for the door. The German *backer* (baker) was still standing in front of the dumbfounded guard, trembling like a leaf, with English cigarettes in his hand.

We left the *backerei*, grabbed the shovel and the pail, and headed back to the camp. As the German unlocked the gate and let us in, I turned to Jim and asked, "What about the fireboxes?"

He chuckled, "There's nothing wrong with them anyway," and he dumped the pail of clay in the yard. Owing to this, Jim Mawbey, Red Perry, and I had a plentiful Christmas, 1943.

One day, out in the bush, Jock Cook and another Dunkirk Scottish lad he was working with got their crosscut saw jammed in a tree they were cutting. Just as the *ober-fester* arrived, one of them said, "I'll get the damn thing out!"

He hit the saw with an axe and knocked about ten inches of teeth out of it. The *ober-fester* screamed "sabotage!" and one hell of an argument started. He wore a green uniform and a hat with a feather in it. Again, I was reminded of Robin Hood, except this man carried a double-barrelled shotgun and had the authority to shoot anyone at any time without asking any questions. Both the Scots were able to speak German fairly well. As we had a bonfire burning to keep warm, the *ober-fester* was on one side of the fire and the two Scots on the other. The *ober-fester* had the shotgun aimed at the one Scotsman's stomach across the fire, which by now had burned down to a pile of red-hot embers. All of a sudden, the two took a step back and the *ober-fester*, not looking down, stepped right into the fire. The men were extremely defiant and brave. These two chaps ended up being charged with sabotage for willfully damaging the property of the beloved Führer.

Later on, a British prisoner was shot and killed out on the job when an argument started about the hours the men were working. He was an innocent bystander sitting on a stump, and was not involved in the argument.

Also at Poppelau were female prisoners working in the bush, watched by guards armed with bullwhips. It was very hard for us to see these poor women, mostly Russians, dressed in rags and slaving out in the cold.

John Chapman of the Calgary Tanks, was quick at catching chickens. On one occasion we had been allowed into the German barn to put fresh straw into our mattresses. There were chickens running around, and like a flash Chapman grabbed a chicken and stuffed it into the palliasse with the straw, right under the noses of the Germans. On another occasion, while walking through a small village on the way to work, a chicken ran across the road behind the guard and in front of Chapman. He grabbed it and stuffed it inside his tunic, trying to stop the chicken from squawking.

On Christmas Eve, someone stole a turkey and hid it underneath a garbage pail inside the compound. The Germans searched everywhere but never thought to look underneath the overturned garbage pail. Some of the men had a delicious turkey for Christmas dinner.

We put together a Christmas concert for ourselves. Several German officers and guards asked if it was okay for them to watch. The men sang carols, acted out some skits, and at the end we sang "God Save the King" as everyone stood up ... including the Germans! After the anthem ended, the Germans asked what we were singing. Someone explained that this was a song we sang every Christmas to our *Gros Gott* ("Big God"). This was accepted.

One day, Philip, the *meister*, pulled from his pocket a folded map of a part of Alberta showing a huge area of ranch country that included what was known as the Prince of Wales Ranch. This was to be his prize, when the Germans had won the war, for his faithfulness to the Führer. He said that he had grown to like my friend Red Perry and that if he had his name and number, he would claim him at the war's end to serve on his ranch, but he could not prevent him from being sterilized. Red Perry's reply was that the Germans would never win the war, and even if they did they would have to shoot him before he would agree to such a proposal.

At this working party, there were two separate rooms, a *tag zimmer* (day room) and a *schlafen zimmer* (sleeping room). After I had been there a few weeks, I teamed up with Bob Laurie of the Queen's Own Cameron Highlanders from Roblin, Manitoba. We knew we would have trouble escaping from the sleeping room, as it faced the German guard room, so we decided to dig a short tunnel to the day room. We cut a hole in the wooden floor of the sleeping room and tunnelled underground until the tunnel reached the outside of the front door of the day room. At the door was a boot scraper, which consisted of several 1 x 3s nailed in a an upright position with spaces in between. We put a bottom in the scraper, boxed it in, attached hinges, and hooked it from the inside. It looked exactly the same as it had before. This was the exit of the tunnel.

The tunnel was completed sometime in March 1944. After it

was finished, other POWs would use the tunnel — not to escape, but to go down to the village. Some of the men had made acquaintances with civilians in the village, and one had a German girl there. We didn't mind the others using the tunnel, as long as it was kept secret from the Germans until we'd made our escape.

With the tunnel completed, we had to decide when to make the break as we had had very little snow, which meant conditions were ideal. (Had there been snow, we would be leaving tracks during our escape.) We planned to head for the Russian front. Unfortunately, the night we had planned to go, we got six to eight inches of snow and we were forced to put our escape plans on hold. Before we got another chance, a German officer arrived at this working party and informed us that all Canadians were to be returned to Stalag VIIIB. Once there, we were to be moved again to a new camp at Stargard. By the time we arrived back at Stalag VIIIB, the other Canadians had already been moved. Consequently, we were never sent to Stalag IID at Stargard.

So we left the tunnel completed and unused. Later on, I heard that the British Commando Sergeant Woodhead, who was in charge of the prisoners at this working party, had been caught in the tunnel and was shot and killed. He had been a great chap. This was a sad ending to *Arbeits Kommando* #164.

Thirteen

Peiskretscham

In May of 1944, the men were suddenly moved, for no apparent reason, from the Dieppe compound to the working compound, which was closer to the main gate and where the bed bugs seemed worse than ever. Shortly afterwards, they found themselves forming a working party and marching out the gates to a place called Peiskretscham, near Hindenburg. Their job was to construct a cement culvert underneath a huge railway yard to let traffic go underneath. This was not war work. Jack's friend Ian Gilmour had once again changed over his identity, this time with a Dieppe Canadian, so that the two of them could plan another escape together.

We arrived back at Stalag VIIIB around the middle of February 1944, and were put back in the Dieppe compound, which was now empty and cold. In a way, it was sad that the Canadians had all gone and it was expected that we would follow them. However, this didn't happen.

Three months later we were moved to the working compound, hut 35A, where a year earlier I had exchanged identities with George Jones. While here, we were often grabbed for work details around the camp. Early in May, they told us we were being sent out to a work party. Ian Gilmour had joined me after changing over with a Canadian, and we both thought this could be another opportunity to escape. We left Stalag VIIIB, going through the regular checking and searching. We were then marched to the railway station at Lamsdorf. Here we were put into the famous cattle trucks for the free ride to Peiskretscham, *Arbeits Kommando #357*.

The job was located about three kilometres from the camp. On our way each day, we would pass a school. The teacher and the children would dance around the flag pole singing one of the German songs of hate. Whenever they came to the word England, they would all spit in unison. We thought this was quite comical and would applaud. We put vile and obscene words to their songs of hate and would sing them in German when marching through a village or town. This would infuriate the civilians.

One day on the way to the job, a German officer, accompanied by several other ranks, stopped our column and told our guard that we were to unload several German Tiger tanks that had been disabled on the Russian Front, as they needed the flat cars to take replacements back. A ferocious argument ensued between the Germans and our interpreters, as we blatantly refused to do this because it was war work. All the tanks seemed to have been hit in the same place — between the tracks low down — leaving a hole. While the argument continued, one of the smaller men crawled inside a tank to steal the headsets. The argument went on for several hours. The words "Geneva Convention" kept coming up. Eventually, the officer gave up and we continued on our way to the job.

My first act of sabotage at Peiskretscham was to deliberately break three shovel handles in a row over the rail of the track. The Germans were furious, screaming "sabotage!" They took my name and number. However, the rest of the prisoners that were present all lined up and gave their names and numbers. On arrival back at the camp that evening, the German sergeant came looking for "Polton, #26212." They had changed the spelling of my name and told me I had been spelling it wrong all along. The other prisoners convinced the sergeant that if they charged me, they would have to charge them all. At least thirty men had given their names and numbers. The charge must have been dropped as I did not hear any more about it.

A day or two later, while I was out on the job, they came looking for someone who could drive a team of horses. A young Royal Navy chap who knew I had been raised on a farm pointed to me and said innocently that I could. The German's face lit up and he said, "*das iz gud*" (that is good), but to his surprise, I said no. I told him "I will use my back, but not my brain for the Fatherland." I still flatly refused even after they promised me some goodies, such as being allowed into the town and maybe in somewhere for a beer or two.

Peiskretscham was a very large rail centre. Trains to and from the Russian front were continually going through. There were trains coming back loaded with wounded soldiers and disabled Tiger and Panther tanks. Also, there were many trains going one way with cattle trucks full of people: men, women, and children. These trains all seemed to be heading in the direction of Poland. There would be hands clawing at the bars on the ventilation openings and voices begging for water. They would stare at us with pleading eyes. We were not aware at this time that these unfortunate souls, being Hungarian Jews, were on their way to a death camp.

At times we would have to walk some distance along the railway. I would step in between the freight cars, uncouple the air hose, remove the rubber seal, re-couple the hose then discard the rubber seal. I probably removed at least fifty of these seals over a period of time. This would render the air brakes on the train useless, and hopefully cause an accident. My airman friend, Ian Gilmour, had changed over with a Dieppe Canadian, Bob Laurie of the Queen's Own Cameron Highlanders from Roblin, Manitoba. I knew him well, as we planned an escape together from a working party at a place called Poppelau in Poland in the winter of 1944.

Gilmour and I made a habit of removing the oil-soaked packing that lubricated the axle bearings on the freight cars (cattle trucks). He would lift the cover, reach in, and pull out the packing and I would throw in handfuls of crushed rock to replace it. This would burn out the bearing after a few miles. Some of the packing we would use for fuel; the rest would be discarded. Many things had to be in our favour in order to do this. Sometimes we would be walking between two rows of cars. This made it easier, as did the fact that some of the guards weren't too bright. There was a type of steel wedge called a wheel chock to hold the cars on the siding from moving. Several times I placed one of these on the main line, hoping to cause a derailment.

One day we did not want the soup that was brought out to the job and decided to give it to the Russian prisoners who were working nearby. The German guard that was with the Russians screamed that it was forbidden to give our soup to the Russians. A terrible argument erupted with our interpreter, Perry, saying that "We will do as we damn well please with our soup!"

Meanwhile, a half-starved Russian had dived into the *kubel* with his bare hands and was forcing the hot soup into his mouth, scalding his hands and face. The German guard grabbed the Russian by the neck and pulled him out, upsetting the soup. The Russians began eating the soup off the ground. There were women prisoners, mostly Russian, slaving on the railway. The women were barefoot and had to push the crushed rock under the ties with bare hands to raise the track. The guards were armed with bullwhips.

June 6, 1944, we finally got the long-awaited news that the second front had opened. I saw my friend Red Perry in a huddle with a Pole. The Pole was talking very rapidly in German. Perry walked over to where I was standing with several other men and said, "I have just been told British and American forces landed successfully in France at 06:00 this morning."

We took the news very calmly. There was no jubilation shown: we knew that the Germans were a formidable force, and we could only hope that the landings would help us win the war.

That evening the German sergeant of the guard called us together and confirmed that Allied forces had landed on the coast of France. I wondered why he bothered to tell us.

The main reason for the working party at Peiskretscham was to construct an underpass under the many railway lines. The work was being done by a Dutch contractor, named Raiderman. He was as bad as the Germans; a proper swine.

As this happened to be an industrial area of Germany, we saw several United States air raids, each made up of at least a thousand bombers. As a raid was taking place one day, Ian Gilmour exclaimed as he looked up in the sky, "I'll be damned, they've got a fighter escort!" This was probably the first time a fighter escort was used this deep into Germany. The allies had finally gotten the long-range Mustang, which could fly a long distance and still have fuel for fighting.

The German anti-aircraft guns would all go off simultaneously. The whole earth would shake. We would take cover under the culvert that we were constructing and we could hear the large chunks of shrapnel hitting the earth. When we commented on these incredible air raids, the Germans would say that they were German planes. We would retort, "German planes bombing Germany?"

At the job site there were two large cement mixers and two concrete pumps, all powered by electric motors. The concrete pumps would push the cement through a six-inch pipe, up to the forms where some of the prisoners were supposed to be tamping the cement down to get all the air out. When the first section was finished and the forms removed, there were cement bags and pieces of timber that had been deliberately left in the forms. I had planned to sabotage one of the concrete pumps. The cement from the mixer was dumped through a type of screen before it reached the pump. I had half-filled a cement bag with bolts, railway spikes, and other items, and when given an all clear signal by a chap named Tremblay from the FMRs (Les Fusiliers Mont-Royal), I raised the screen and threw the bag in. It only took a few minutes, and the pump ground to a halt as the bolts and spikes reached the cylinder and jammed the piston. This meant that all the pipes that stretched for about two hundred feet had to be taken apart and the cement cleaned out. This would cause a long delay and a lot of wasted cement. However, they switched over to the other concrete pump and the work continued. Back at the camp that evening, I went around scrounging sugar. The next morning, unseen, I poured the sugar into the oil cups of the electric motor that powered the cement mixer. As the heat melted the sugar, it ran through to the bearings and seized the motor. They were able to remove the motor from the other mixer and after a few hours delay, the work continued. So I finally gave up.

Eventually I stopped these pranks when I realized the Polish slave workers were being blamed for things I had done. There were many Poles there at the time, and they were being forced to work twelve-hour shifts. (We, meanwhile, had been able to get our hours cut down to ten, though it took a terrible row with the Germans to get this break.)

Several other incidents took place at this working party. On one occasion we were unloading crushed rock from a railway car when a locomotive arrived with a train crew. Gilmour, who could speak the language, heard them mention that they needed this car to ship tanks to the Russian front. We dropped the shovels and refused to finish unloading the car. A terrible argument erupted. They made all kinds of threats, and even said they would shoot us if we did not get back to work. Regardless, we sat down and were still out there until dark. Finally, they decided to take us back to the camp.

The highlight of my exploits came one afternoon. There was a narrow gauge railway track crossing a main road, which was used to transport war materials to and from the Russian front. This road was crucial to the German war effort. The track had to be uncoupled and swung around periodically, clear of the road, to let traffic through. The train cars were used to move fill from one side of the road to a job that was being done on the other side, and were pulled by a small donkey engine. This particular afternoon, a mini train was crossing the main road just as a German convoy of trucks was arriving, headed for the Russian front. In a split second I picked up a piece of two-inch plank about five feet long and threw it under the wheels of one of the cars. This caused several of the cars to jump the track. Many of the German truck drivers left their trucks with the engines still running and walked closer to have a look at what was happening. By coincidence, a convoy of German staff cars arrived from the opposite direction. A German general displaying much braid and decoration got out of the lead car, screaming to clear the road immediately. Red Perry, who was acting as our interpreter, waved us back and said "don't touch a thing, but stick together."

Seeing that the prisoners of war were not going to obey his command, the general went into a frenzy and resembled a mad man. He was red in the face, with great beads of sweat on his forehead, and was foaming at the mouth, demanding that we get the cars back on the track or he would have us all shot. The only funny thing that happened there that day was the truck drivers bolting back to their trucks. This was probably the first time this German general had ever been refused an order. Everyone, including the people in the cars, appeared terrified of this man. It was tough to have to watch the Poles having to manually put the cars back on the track, but we had sworn not to do anything that would aid the German war effort and had no intention of breaking that promise. What I had done caused at least three hours delay in both convoys. This may seem insignificant, but to have been there and witnessed this gave me a good feeling. However, it was a miracle that no one was shot. Apparently, no one saw me throw the plank.

I noticed that there were women in both cars and trucks. It seemed the Germans always had women with them.

Ian Gilmour and I had gone out on this work party for the sole purpose of escaping. During the evenings and weekends, we dug a tunnel. The entrance was under the bunk of my friend Red Perry. Earlier a tunnel had been discovered in the camp and it was suspected that there was a German agent among us.

We hid some civilian clothes down on the job in readiness. Mine included a pair of Wellington rubber boots, a pair of dark blue coveralls and a civilian cap. The idea was that we would disguise ourselves as German workers. I planned to put the coveralls on over my uniform so that, if we were caught, I could quickly take the coveralls off and be recognized as an escaped POW. If I were caught disguised as a worker, with nothing to identify me as an escaped POW, they would assume I was a spy. A spy would receive far greater punishment than an escaped POW.

We hoped that we could get on a train and make it to the Russian front, as freight trains would slow down or sometimes stop as they were going through. We felt we had a good chance of getting on one of them.

As we had to move Red Perry's bunk to get at the tunnel entrance, he was awake and a witness to what happened that night. There was a window in the hut just to the right of the tunnel. At about 23:00 hours, when we had decided to leave, we could see the chest and part of the rifle of a German soldier against the wall standing on top of the tunnel. He was watching where we would come up outside the fence under a water tank. We came to the conclusion that someone had found out that there was a tunnel and had given it away. Therefore, there must be a traitor or a German agent in the camp. The following Sunday morning, the Germans rushed in, pulled Perry's bunk out and found the tunnel entrance. That night, Red Perry suggested that we give up the attempt: it wasn't worth risking being shot now that the second front had started — the war might be over in a few months. Reluctantly, we took his advice.

During the summer after the Normandy landings on June 6, the German civilians were getting the wind up. With the Russians now making great progress in the east, the civilians would look at us with fear in their eyes and say, "Rouskie come, Rouskie come."

A German electrician working on the job asked Red Perry for

his home address so that he could show it to the Russians when they arrived. He reminded Red that he had been good to the prisoners. By having Red's address, he hoped to show the Russians he had been so good to the prisoners that he had become friends with one of them. However, the request was denied. (The Russians probably wouldn't have been impressed anyways.)

Throughout my ordeal as a POW I continued to suffer from the trench mouth I had contracted while training for the Dieppe raid on the Isle of Wight. As the Germans had no treatment for it, the infection continued to come and go during my time as a prisoner. However, I used this to my advantage.

Since another escape attempt had been foiled, all of the digging on the tunnel wasted, and my patience with working for the Germans at an end, I decided to try to get sent back to Stalag VIIIB. As the trench mouth kept breaking out and the Germans had no cure, I decided to go on their so-called sick parade. First, you had to see a French doctor with a German officer present. The interpreter shoved a few cigarettes in the doctor's pocket and informed him how contagious this was, that it could infect the whole German army. On hearing this, the German officer told the doctor I would have to travel to Gleiwitz, Poland to see the German *zahnarzt* (dentist).

I was sent by train along with several other prisoners and a guard. We arrived at Gleiwitz to find an air raid in progress. On leaving the railway station, we were told by the guard that only the Germans were allowed to walk on the sidewalk in Poland; we were to walk on the street like the Poles. We told him to go to hell, and deliberately walked on the sidewalk. This being my first time in a Polish city, I couldn't believe such disrespect was being shown to the Poles in their own country. I was also shocked that they all had to wear a "P" on their clothing to signify that they were Polish.

There were over one thousand U.S. bombers overhead — it was something to behold. The streets were deserted, and we were taken down under a large building that served as shelter.

After the raid was over, we eventually found the German *zahnarzt*. Having not even looked in my mouth, he agreed that I should be sent back to Stalag VIIIB for the treatment that they didn't have. The trench mouth had finally paid off. For me, this was the end of *Arbeits Kommando* #357 at Peiskretscham.

About a week later, Gilmour, who was using the name Bob Laurie, arrived back as well. I asked him what he had done to get sent in. He pointed to his mouth and said, "No teeth." This surprised me, for he had perfect teeth. Gilmour explained that Jock Cook, a Dunkirk prisoner I had known at Poppelau, had no teeth and had gone to the doctor using Bob Laurie's name and number saying he would not do any more work until he got some teeth. A few days later a German guard arrived, picked up "Bob Laurie" (Ian Gilmour) and returned him to Stalag VIIIB for teeth. Ian asked me to help him find someone in camp who had no teeth and who would report to the German dentist saying that he was Bob Laurie. Once this was done, there was nothing to worry about as it might be months or even longer waiting for teeth.

Gilmour resumed his proper identity and returned to the Air Force compound. We remained in Stalag VIIIB until leaving in January 1945 on what was to become known as The Death March. The foiled escape attempt at Peiskretscham was to be our last attempt together.

The Germans were putting up signs all over the camp warning prisoners that anyone trying to escape would be shot on sight; escaping was no longer a sport. (I didn't know that it ever had been a sport.) I took one of the signs down, and it now hangs in my rec room. I later learned that these signs were a response to the Great Escape, which took place at Stalag Luft III.

During the ensuing months, most of my time was taken up with news of the progress of the Allied troops and the Russian front. We were receiving the BBC news from secret radios. These radios had to be kept secret from the Germans, so we made sure the maps we had drawn on the walls to chart the war always corresponded with news we received from the Germans (which would usually be about four weeks behind), not the news we were hearing on the BBC. Had the Germans seen our up-to-date information, they would know we had radios. In the working compound was a radio which was hidden in the block führer's office. Two Australians had a key and would go in each night to receive the eleven o'clock news from Britain. There was also the

Following the Great Escape at Stalag Luft III, the Germans put up these signs warning prisoners not to attempt to escape.

radio hidden in a piano accordion inside the Air Force compound, on which I listened to the news. Another one was in an underground compartment in what had been the Dieppe compound. The Germans never did find these radios.

The first prisoner captured in Italy to arrive at Stalag VIIIB was Private Barrie of the West Nova Scotia Regiment, First Canadian Division. Barrie was like a breath of fresh air. He brought us first-hand news of the fighting in Italy. It gave us hope that we were finally getting the upper hand. The First Canadian Division had found the German army as formidable a foe as the Second Division had two years earlier. As Barrie was alone among all the men from Second Division, I became friendly with him and we mucked in together. This meant sharing all the Red Cross food that we received in the parcels. He would be in charge and would decide at any particular meal time what we would have to eat. The red patch on his sleeve really stood out among all the blue of Second Division. It was great to have him with us. (I would lose track of Barrie when we left on the Death March in January 1945.)

Our bunks were situated right inside the main door, so whenever the Germans required a working party, we would be chosen. On one occasion I was grabbed to go and shake German blankets that had just been deloused. We were in the dark most of the time and badly needed a light bulb, so while in the German barracks I jumped up on another prisoner's shoulders, reached up, and unscrewed the light bulb while no one was looking. I carried this light bulb back under my hat into the camp, as we were searched going back in. They did not think of looking under my hat. Barrie was really thrilled when I walked back in with the light bulb. This made it all worthwhile.

One day the Germans pulled a raid, breaking up the cement floor and knocking down chimneys looking for a radio. All they found was a decoy that had been planted on purpose. However they failed to search the block führer's office, where the Australians listened to war news on the radio, while someone took down the news in short hand, to be read out later to the prisoners in the other huts.

As the months rolled by, the big American four-engine bombers would fly over almost every day. We hoped they would drop a few bombs on the camp. After 1944, they would have a fighter escort with them. There would be so many aircraft that it was impossible to count them. However, some of the bombers were being hit by anti-aircraft fire. They would come down like wounded birds. One day in particular, we saw nine parachutes open. The following day, the Germans asked for a burial party for nine American airmen.

At night we could hear the British and Canadian bombers overhead, and it seemed we were always on the alert. Near Stalag VIIIB there was a military training area, and we were able to witness many German student pilots crash, which brought a great cheer from hundreds of POWs.

We had been getting news on a regular basis, and up until

December all the news had been relatively good. Then we received the bad news of the German offensive known as the Battle of the Bulge. This German attack was an attempt to split the Allies and advance to the English Channel in order to relieve German troops cut off by the Allies at the Port of Antwerp. The Allies were caught off guard, and suffered terrible casualties and prisoners of war. It was an awful kick in the teeth for to hear this news, after everything had been going so well for our side. Fortunately, the Germans were unsuccessful in their attempt and were defeated.

At about this time, the Russians were sweeping across Poland en masse. We were hoping that any day Russian troops would arrive at the gates. However, in January 1945, the Germans decided that we would evacuate the camp and go out on what was to become known as the Death March. The worst was yet to come!

Fourteen
The Death March

By mid-January 1945, the men of Stalag VIIIB were preparing for the evacuation. They were told to take what they could carry because they were leaving the camp. However, no reason was given.

I hastened to dig up a set of chains I had buried in the working compound. I was determined to bring them back to show everyone what we had gone through for all those months. Along with the chains, I brought a number of items, including: British army boots that I was reluctant to leave behind; one regular blanket; one heavy crocheted blanket made by Harry Smith of the Royals out of scarves and sweaters; an Italian backpack containing one thousand Buckingham cigarettes, which by some miracle I had received that day from my cousin, Sylvia Floyd of Toronto; a quarter of a pound of Salada tea that my mother had sent in my last comfort parcel; and of course, one of the English Red Cross Christmas parcels, which had arrived late and were handed out at the gate as we departed, one to a man. They were frozen solid. I tried to gnaw on a frozen Christmas pudding that was as hard as concrete.

The evacuation ran over two days. I went out on the second day. Although there were airmen on my column, this is where I lost contact with Ian Gilmour. Sadly, I never saw him again.

As we walked away from Stalag VIIIB, I didn't even turn around to have a last look. The weather was below zero, and there were banks of snow up to four feet high along the side of the road. We passed many men who had frozen to death the day before on the side of the road. Seeing these frozen bodies reminded me of the four-foot logs that had fallen off trucks on the icy roads of my hometown.

After about fifteen miles, I began to tire as I was carrying more than I could handle. Eventually, I leaned against a snow bank on the side of the road, and slid to a sitting position. A German officer arrived on the scene, put a pistol to my temple and said, "Get up and march, you swine, or be shot." Recalling the frozen dead bodies I had seen that day, I realized that he was quite serious. So I got up and staggered on.

A Scottish prisoner, Jock MacPhee of the Gordon Highlanders, was not carrying any possessions, and I wondered what he had done with his English Red Cross Christmas parcel. He came along side of me and offered to help me carry some of my load. I agreed to share the tea and the cigarettes with him while they lasted. As a result of this, we became close friends.

I will never forget that first night. We had stopped in an open field, where the only structure was a hay shed that had a roof but no walls. After walking in the snow for hours our leather army boots were soaked. Many men took their wet boots off to dry. The next morning, the column of prisoners was starting to move off, with some men still trying desperately to get frozen boots onto their feet. They built a fire to try to thaw their boots out, but it was quickly stomped out by the Germans. I recall some of the men starting out walking in the snow in their socks, carrying their frozen boots. We learned that it was best to leave our boots on and let them freeze on our feet. I had an extra pair of socks my mother had sent, and when we would stop for the night, I would take each boot off and very quickly change my sock and put the boot back on before it could freeze. I would put the wet socks against my stomach, inside my tunic, to dry from the heat of my body.

We were very lucky that we all had greatcoats but many didn't have gloves or mitts. There were days when the mucus in our nose would be frozen. As well, the moisture in our eyes would freeze.

One very cold night in an open field, several airmen were huddled together in the snow on the frozen ground, trying to sleep. I kept warning them not to go to sleep as their feet would surely freeze. I spent that night doubling on the spot and clapping my arms in order to keep warm. In the morning, these airmen were unable to stand as their feet had frozen during the night.

For the next few months, it was every man for himself. You had to keep moving or be shot. For several days, we were between the Russian front line and the German second line of defence. All of the Germans' equipment was painted white, and the officers were mounted on white horses. The roads were backed up with civilians evacuating. German tanks were driving over horses and wagons. These were their own people they were driving over! This was just one of the many horrible things we were to witness before the march was over.

After a few days, we entered a POW camp at Gorlitz (Stalag VIIIA). This was like a living nightmare. The first thing I saw as we entered the gates was a member of my own regiment who had been confined in a wire cage, probably as a punishment for escaping. People were in mud up to their knees, and we received no food of any kind while we were there. A black American soldier kept singing "Paper Dolly" over and over. Vivid memories of Gorlitz have instilled a deep-seated hatred of the song ever since.

After several days at Gorlitz, we proceeded on our way, covering twenty-five to thirty kilometres a day. After a few weeks on the march, people were discarding things on the wayside: musical instruments, blankets, and other bits and pieces of gear. I remember seeing a chap who really played the accordion well smashing it against a fence post. It must have been terrible for a musician to have to destroy his instrument. As for me, I had carried the chains for miles until I realized that I might not even make it back home again, so there was no point carrying the chains anymore. I threw them into a field.

One day, I grabbed a can of milk which had been left on the side of the road for the trucks to pick up. Luckily, I had my mug wired to my belt and dipped it in. I backed away to drink the cupful of milk, and while other prisoners were scrambling to get at the can, a German guard came rushing in and hit one man over the back with his rifle so hard he broke the rifle in half. I'll never forget his face as he stood with a piece of his rifle in either hand. I assumed he was wondering how he would explain this to his officer.

We overtook inmates of a concentration camp being herded down the road dressed in their striped prison clothes, some of them in bare feet. The Germans had them pulling a team wagon loaded with the Germans' equipment, some pulling with pieces of rope or wire and others pushing from behind. It was a nightmare just to see these people. We were unable to look them in the eye. It was probable that these people were from Auschwitz. It made one feel humble knowing that if it wasn't for the uniform we were wearing, we might have been in the same state.

At one stop along the way, a German officer asked if any of the men wished to see a German doctor. I stepped out, as my heel was rubbed raw and I was limping. The German doctor decided that I would be one of twelve who were picked out of about eight hundred. We were taken by a guard to a German military hospital, led up five flights of stairs to the attic, and ushered into a room. As I was the only one that knew enough German to converse, I pleaded with the guard to at least try to get us some soup, which he eventually did. No doctor or any medical person came near us. The next morning, a German sergeant arrived, saying that we had to leave immediately and head for the next town, which was about twenty-five kilometres away. That was my only experience in a German hospital. I believe we were only offered medical attention for propaganda purposes.

It seemed that, as the end of the war drew nearer, the treatment kept getting worse. They were still adamant that they were winning the war. We had heard about the V1 and V2 rockets, although we had no idea how deadly accurate they were. We were shocked to hear the talk about the V3, which was a rocket that could reach North America. The Germans kept telling us that, with this weapon, they could still win the war.

Many escape attempts were made along the way. Quite frequently we would hear a shot, knowing that someone had been caught. As for myself, I kept waiting for the perfect moment.

We continued to walk twenty-five to thirty kilometres a day. Many nights were spent in open fields or in farmyards, never under cover. With luck we would get a bread ration every fourth or fifth day. As I had been raised on a farm, I knew where to look for things that were edible. On one occasion I found a root cellar where there were potatoes. On another occasion I stole a bucket of swill that was being prepared for pigs. I also stole oats out of a horse's oat box. As the farmer went up one side of the horse and put the oats in the oat box, I went up the other side and scooped them into my hat before the horse got a chance to eat them. I shared everything with two South African brothers, Doug and Harry Brailsford, who I had befriended.

About mid-February, we met up with some of the Americans that had been captured at the Battle of the Bulge. My heart went out to these men, as they were in a terrible state. They had been captured in the winter, six months earlier, and had been civilians in the U.S. We had become accustomed to being POWs, and had the experience of years of army training. We were also fortunate enough to have been captured during warm weather. But these Americans had come from their comfortable lives at home and ended up on this gruelling march, without any preparation to help steel them against the conditions.

There were two Americans dragging their buddy for miles, refusing to let him go even though he had died. Finally, we convinced them that if they did not drop him they would wind up in the same situation.

We were living in fear of disease — typhus and the flu. In World War I, the flu had killed millions — more people died from the flu than from military action. As well, there was the constant danger of being attacked by our own aircraft. Although planes

Doug (left) and Harry Brailsford, back at home in South Africa. Jack befriended these two brothers while on the Death March.

flew over us several times, only once did my column become a target. We were machine-gunned. Several prisoners were killed during this raid. The Germans were the first to hit the ditch.

Two Americans walking behind me were talking about the English bread. One said to the other, "I just have to get back to England and have some more of their bread." I remembered that, while on manoeuvres in England, we would buy loaves of English bread and eat it like cake. This took my mind back to the stale bread that we would pick up from the bakery to feed the chickens on the farm.

Around the beginning of March 1945, I thought it was senseless to go on like this. Being herded into a farmyard after an exhausting day on the road, I decided it was time to make an escape attempt. That night, I was trying to sleep amidst the noise of starving men's moans and groans and the horrible stench, and I dozed off. I awoke suddenly and felt someone untying my boots. I could make out a figure in the darkness on his knees unlacing my boots. I pulled my two feet back and hit him in the chest, driving him about fifteen feet. He landed on one of the few Canadians among us, a sailor named French, who belted him again.

For my escape, I teamed up with an Australian who was of the same mind as I was. As there were dairy cows in the barn I thought I'd get myself a mug full of milk before leaving as it would give me the energy I needed. After asking the Australian if he would mind waiting, I entered the cow barn through a small sliding door. This, of course, disturbed the cattle. After finding one that I could milk, I filled the mug and was standing drinking the milk when the owner of the farm, a huge man, came in another door and put the lights on. He picked up a broken fork handle and came rushing at me screaming *"schwein hund"* and yelling for the guards that were outside. Luckily, I had almost finished the milk and was able to put my left arm up to ward off the blows as he was aiming for my head. By a miracle, I was able to grab my haversack and water bottle, which I had put down on what appeared to be an oil drum. As I bolted out the door, he hit me across the back with the fork handle, causing me to lose my breath. In the dark, I stumbled over a piece of farm machinery and slid into a pit that held the urine from the cattle in the barn. I was fortunate to go in feet first, but as I had my four-day ration of black bread in my great coat pocket, the bread was ruined. When the farmer came out the door screaming for the guards, who were running around with flashlights looking for me, I was hidden in the pit where I couldn't be seen. I sprang out of the pit and dove through a doorway that led to a set of stairs going to the loft, where I discovered several other prisoners sleeping. I dove head first into a pile of straw and pulled myself in until my boots were hidden. After some time I managed to fall asleep. By morning, I had dried off somewhat.

In the morning we were lined up so the farmer could pick out the Englander *schwein* he had caught in the barn. As I had been wearing a hat and greatcoat, I rolled up the coat and laid it at another man's feet and asked someone else to wear my hat. He and several German officers went up and down the lines of prisoners. He passed me several times, not recognizing me. I was glad the farmer hadn't seen me in the pit. Had he known I was in there, he would have been able to identify me by smell alone.

I heard the farmer remark to the German officers that the prisoner must have *vickloffed* (run away). This had been a close call.

I have no idea what happened to the Australian. The thought passed through my mind many times that, had stayed with the Australian and not stopped to go into the barn, we might have made a successful escape.

As the march progressed, we would stagger along, staring at the back of the man ahead. Men were getting thinner and dying by the wayside from exhaustion and malnutrition. Everyone was covered with lice. To fall by the wayside meant being shot. As I had not had my clothes off or washed or shaved for nearly three months, things were getting worse every day. The only way we could quench our thirst was to drink out of the ditch at the side of the road. It was a test of determination for one to survive. All that kept us going were the memories of our loved ones so far away.

For days I helped Harry, the South African, drag his brother Doug along, as leaving him would have meant certain death for the poor man. I gladly did this and waived any thanks as it could just as easily have been my brother that needed help. Harry would keep saying that I had saved his brother's life. They begged me to return to South Africa with them and become an equal partner in their construction business.

Hunger was getting so bad that men were picking up rotten turnips and sugar beets along the way and drinking water that was left from the melting snow in the ditch. Day after day, the column of starving men moved on like ghostly figures, barely putting one foot in front of the other, but we were heading west and every step was a step in the right direction. We were on the way home.

As I was still carrying the compass from one of my escape attempts, I would keep checking our direction, yelling this out to the other men. Some of them would say, "How the hell does he know which way we're going?"

The Death March started just west of the Oder River and continued westward across the Elbe River as far west as the Weser River. As we were getting dangerously close to the Western Allied front, the Germans turned us around and headed us back east toward the Elbe.

We stopped for several days at a Brick Factory in Duderstat. Here I traded the ring that had been given to me by my Dad — the ring he had worn in the First World War and that I had kept hidden from the Germans when I was first captured at Dieppe. A German soldier offered me a quarter of a loaf a bread for the ring. Reluctantly, I removed it and took the bread. I shared this with Doug and Harry.

One night, being so lousy, I removed and discarded my underwear and socks in an attempt to get rid of the lice. I put my uniform and boots back on over bare skin. Ten minutes later it was as bad as ever. The lice were sucking the blood out of our bodies. I was scarred all over with lice bites.

Near Duderstat, there was a small river. Men pleaded with the Germans to let them go down to wash at this river, but it was forbidden. Men would be continually killing lice in the crotch of their pants. If you held your socks up to the sun, it would look like an ant hill. You could see the lice moving in the socks. The men died like flies at Duderstat. The place was a nightmare. They were continually coming and asking for burial parties to bury dead comrades.

During our stay here, there was a rumour that American forces had bypassed us on both sides and that we were in a horseshoe. This was why the Germans decided to take us back east towards the Elbe River; they were going to hang onto us to the very end. Many of the men had dysentery and human waste was running through the floor boards from the levels above. It was everywhere in the yard. We accepted this as just one of the many terrible things that were happening.

One rainy day we had been herded into a farmyard with our clothes wet and freezing. That night I entered the barn — an act that was forbidden — and slept between two oxen with long horns who were lying back to back. By the morning, I was warm and rested and my clothes had dried. When the Germans discovered me, I had to flee outside and intermingle with the other men so they couldn't identify me.

I was still carrying the pair of brand-new British army boots that I thought I might need on the way. However, as I grew weaker, I decided that it was time to get rid of the boots. I told my friend, Jock MacPhee from Inverness Scotland, that I still had some tea left. As he had been captured at Dunkirk, a member of the Fifty-First Highland Division, and spoke pretty good German, I suggested that he take the tea and the boots and a small pot that I had wired to my belt, and trade the boots for some boiling water. He came back minus the boots, with lukewarm water and the tea floating on top. That was the end of the boots and the tea.

Throughout the march, we survived on a piece of black bread so small it would equal about four of our slices. This would be issued every three or four days. As the snow melted, the bread would be supplemented by rotten turnips and sugar beets found along the way.

Animal instincts were starting to show and there was a survival-of-the-fittest attitude prevailing. While still on the Death March early in April 1945, the Germans allowed us into a barn one rainy day. This was only the third time we had been under cover in nearly three months. There were at least 150 to 200 prisoners from all parts of the Commonwealth in the barn. We were expecting that the Germans would soon clear us out and get us back on the terrible march. About mid-morning, the barn door opened and in came a German soldier with two British prisoners, one being helped along by the other. He was half-dragged to where there was a wooden box near the centre of the barn. They sat him on the box, facing in my direction. The other British chap informed us that this man had been caught stealing someone's ration in another barn and had been brought here for his own safety. They both left, leaving him sitting there. He was small in stature and wore a greatcoat. He was in a state of shock, bleeding from the nose and mouth. His eyes were almost closed. To this day, I still can remember a lump on his forehead the size of an egg. Almost immediately, men started getting up and advancing towards him. The thought raced through my mind that they were intending to beat him some more. I sprang to my feet, covering the distance of about sixteen feet in a few strides, unbuttoning my greatcoat on the way, trying to look as big and as menacing as possible. He winced as I approached him, thinking I was about to cast the first blow. Instead, I spun around and shouted, "Stop! Don't anyone lay a hand on him. He has had enough. You will have to take me first and I have not stolen anything."

My head was turning from side to side as men were approaching from three directions. I shouted, "You've all been tempted to steal at some time, but never had the guts."

My sudden action must have shocked them as they all stopped and stood there, eventually wandering back to where they had been sitting. This was a great relief to me, for there were at least fifteen or more of them advancing. None of the other men in the barn had made a move, but I would have stood my ground even if they had. Something told me that morning that I must defend this unfortunate man regardless of whether or not he was guilty of stealing. He never spoke to me and I didn't know his name.

As we left the barn shortly thereafter, I have no idea what became of him. He was left behind. This was the second time I had witnessed anyone accused of stealing while I was a prisoner. I did not agree with what had been done to him. It must have been terrible to have your own turn on you. In spite of the danger I put myself in, and the terrible conditions that existed, I have no regrets about my actions.

When we went to sleep, there was snow and when we woke up, the snow had gone. It seemed as though a miracle had happened.

We overtook a German circus on the road. The circus had been travelling on sleighs in the snow. With the snow melted and the runners on the bare road, they were stopped. They tried to get us to push the huge caravans. However, after quite an argument, we refused and continued on. As we left, we could see them getting the elephants to push instead.

On April 11, 1945, the column of prisoners were marched across fields as all the roads were blocked with German tanks and trucks retreating from the Allies to the west. A prisoner asked a boy of about twelve years old to get him some water. The boy came back with the water and a German soldier set upon him, knocking him down, spilling the water and almost kicking him to death. This is how they treated their own people. The prisoners were yelling for him to stop.

As the war neared its end, the Germans became more sadistic. I can't recall one instance where civilians or military people showed any sign of pity or sympathy for the condition we were in.

Fifteen
The Morning I Saw the Angels

On April 11, 1945, the exhausted prisoners staggered into the little town of Ditfurt. They were met with extreme hostility as Allied planes had strafed the town that day, and there were dead bodies and animal carcasses littering the streets. They were herded into a barnyard where they were to spend the night and would have to be ready to march again the next day.

About mid-afternoon on April 11, 1945, we entered the town of Ditfurt. The Germans told us that we would receive no bread, as Allied planes had strafed the town that day. We had eaten nothing for four days. I tried to swap a sweater with a German soldier for some bread. He curtly told me my sweater was "lousy" and walked away.

Knowing where to find things on a farm, I got into the granary and filled my pockets with wheat. I shared this with my two South African friends and a New Zealander.

That evening, I was able to jump up and lean over a wall. A Serbian prisoner walking past the farm told me in German that the Americans were just ten kilometres away and pointed down the road. He added, "They should arrive by 06:00." I asked him where he was going. He said the Americans had captured the farm where he was a prisoner, and he just walked away.

I was afraid to believe what I had heard. I stood there trying to take in what he had said. I was elated, I went from man to man trying to tell them the good news. Many of them were too far gone to understand what I was saying and others showed a disinterest.

I decided this might be a good chance to attempt an escape as I had found a way to get out. I did not want to go alone. I had found out it was terrible to be a prisoner and alone. The South African would not leave his brother and my New Zealand friend said to me, "I would only hold you back, Canada. I am too far gone." I believe he died during the night.

I had a hard time falling asleep, wondering if what the Serbian had said was the truth. Were the Americans really only ten kilometres away? We had heard no sounds of gunfire. I was awakened on the morning of the 12th at about 06:00 by a rooster crowing. Harry was shouting from the barnyard, "There's a jeep out there! There's a jeep out there!"

Two large doors on the barnyard were ajar, guarded by two German soldiers. I got to my feet, ran through, and there, almost in the centre of Germany, was a jeep and three American soldiers. I saw three angels that morning. It was like coming back from the dead. We were liberated. I will never forget that day.

I stood there staring at the white star on the hood, almost afraid that it was an illusion, and if I looked away, it would disappear. The white star symbolized to me goodness and decency, quite a contrast to the evil that surrounded us.

There was an officer, a driver, and a radio operator. These liberators were the American troops that were to meet the Russians at the Elbe River, the Second Armoured Regiment of the Ninth United States Army. Other men were crowding around the jeep. One actually broke his leg on the bumper as he rushed it. Men's tears were leaving little trails in the dust on the hood. The radio operator kept repeating, "Do not fire on this town. I repeat, do not fire on this town. There are Yanks and Tommies here." He was radioing back to the advancing American armour. They had discovered us in the nick of time.

I saluted and asked the officer where he was from and mentioned that I was from Toronto. He told me he was from Ohio. I told him that we had seen German armoured units in the immediate area the day before. As he got back into the jeep, he informed us that their tanks would arrive in about fifteen minutes. My eyes filled with tears as I watched the jeep disappear through the winding streets of the town. Then, remembering that I was still a soldier, I walked smartly toward the nearest German, who was still guarding the doors, and relieved him of his rifle and bayonet. He said to me, "*Ich bin ein gefangener jetzt.*" (I am the prisoner now.)

Did I want revenge? No. We were all too sick and ill to want revenge. Only when a German had gone out of his way to be extra cruel to the prisoners might he be singled out for revenge. I had been trained to kill the enemy when he was armed and trying to kill me, not after he had handed over his weapon.

The German was hoping to follow me around, which might save him from being shot by the Americans. Needless to say, I got rid of him as I had other things on my mind. I went back to the barnyard carrying the German rifle and told my friend Doug what had happened. He just stared at me, offering no response. I shoved the rifle under some straw and went back outside and down the street where I had seen a bakery. I rushed in and grabbed two loaves of black bread off the rack. On the way back, there was a milk truck stopped on the side of the road. I grabbed one of the smaller cans of milk and returned to the barnyard. Leaving this with the two South Africans I went back out to await the arrival of the American tanks. Standing with a sergeant of the Irish Guards, we saluted our liberators as their Sherman tanks rolled by, laden with infantry men. What a sight to behold. Here I was witnessing something I thought I could only dream of seeing. As these American soldiers began to cheer us, we removed our hats in respect for the men who had just given us back our freedom.

By coincidence, my friend Jock MacPhee had taken the other guard prisoner and to my surprise, the two of them were walking up the street, both in step, MacPhee armed with the rifle. He had the German going from door to door, hoping to find someone who would give them breakfast. The German asked MacPhee to take him to Scotland.

Later that day, the American troops offered to give us their day's ration. This we refused, but we gratefully accepted their cigarettes. The generosity of these troops was unbelievable. The American commanding officer, upon viewing the state of the men in the barnyard, ordered his medical team to take over and look after the worst cases immediately. He called his officers to come and look upon these people, saying, "Now we know how they treat their prisoners."

It was hard to pick out the dead from the dying. Those of us who were still fit enough had formed a unit with "Kippy," a South African RSM who had acted as our interpreter and leader. With many of the men able to speak German, we offered to go on with the American forces to try to help in any way we could. They said that they appreciated our offer, but explained that if they agreed to the proposal, "Ike would have their heads." They added that they thought we had been through enough and they would take care of everything. They advised us to arm ourselves with German weapons, and gave us permission to search houses and bring in prisoners by flushing out Germans who had shed their uniforms for civilian clothes. They said that only British, American, and Commonwealth ex-prisoners would be allowed to carry arms. By allowing us to do these things, they helped to restore our dignity.

The German officer in command of our column handed Kippy a paper. The paper contained orders signed by Heinrich Himmler, dated April 11, that no prisoners were to be found alive. Everyone was to be shot. Obviously, this officer had disobeyed an order. He probably did this to save his own skin.

One of my duties was to guard the town hall along with a Scot, an American, and two South Africans. The Scottish chap took the German flag down, folded it up, and put it inside his tunic. I managed to get a smaller flag that was up on a wall in the town hall. Confiscated cameras and weapons of all kinds had been brought to this hall. There were rooms full of Lugers, rifles, machine guns, and mortar shells. American soldiers would come looking for Lugers and shotguns and would ask us if it was okay if they went in to pick out a weapon. After liberating us they still saw fit to ask if it was okay.

I already had a Luger, which I'd taken from beside the body of the town S.S. leader, who had committed suicide. I later traded the Luger to an American soldier for twenty Chesterfield cigarettes. He had first offered me sixty American dollars, which I turned down. I would have given it to him for nothing.

After months of starvation and horrible living conditions, things were finally changing for the better, and the American commanding officer issued an order to the *burgermeister* (mayor) that they were to make soup twice a day for all the liberated prisoners.

I spent my first night of freedom in a German house with an

American tank crew. I listened to stories the sergeant told about losing fifteen tanks since the D-Day landings. All of a sudden, firing broke out and I could distinctly hear a Bren gun being fired. As the Germans had been using captured Bren guns guarding the prisoners, the liberated men had reclaimed these Bren guns and were out on patrol with the American forces. While this firing was occurring, I heard a voice out in the street say, "Drivers, start your engines, and all vehicles prepare to move." I said to the American sergeant, "If your tank moves, I don't care what direction it's going, I am going to be on it. The bastards are not going to get me again." He made no reply.

It turned out that a patrol of S.S. and Hitler Youth had tried to penetrate the town and had been detected, thus causing the firing in the streets. (Later we heard that liberated prisoners had been murdered in barns by Hitler Youth penetrating liberated territory.) After a short while, and much to my relief, I heard the engines being shut down. The tanks did not move that night.

The next day we would hear the sad news that President Roosevelt had died.

Two days later, two German women came to the town hall, begging for someone to go and sleep in their houses, as they were being threatened by renegade Poles who were running loose in the area. They asked if a British or American "comrade" would go and sleep in their house at night to protect them. They said they would wash our clothes and feed us. One of these women was pregnant and actually got down on her knees and begged the Scottish interpreter. The American officer said, "It's up to you boys. I don't care whether you do it or not. But if you agree, they will have to do your washing and cooking for you."

We agreed to go with them. For five nights, we all slept in different German households. The house I was in contained a woman, two small children, and an older woman who I assumed was the woman's mother. They cooked me some eggs. I had the German rifle leaning against my thigh as I sat at the table because I wasn't trusting anyone. The two German children kept peeking around a doorway and edging closer and closer to me, finally one reached out and touched me and then sprang back.

Hitler had brainwashed the German people into believing that the British and Americans would rape and pillage if they ever got into Germany. That evening, while sitting at the table in this house, I observed a lot of shuffling going on in one of the bedrooms. The older woman came to me and said in German that I would "*schlaf with the junge frau*" (sleep with the young woman) in the bedroom and she would sleep on the couch in the living room. I guess they believed what Hitler had been telling them, that we wanted their women. I made it quite clear in my best German that I was not interested in the *junge frau* (young woman) and that I would *schlaf* on the couch in the living room.

I slept on the couch with the rifle in the corner and two extra clips of ammunition under my pillow. During the night I woke up violently ill. I thought I had been poisoned. I managed to get a window open and threw up outside. I then realized that I had not been poisoned; it was just that my system could not tolerate food after not having had anything substantial for so long.

After liberation, I recall a German train loaded with supplies that had been abandoned. They had unhooked the locomotive and taken off. A group of liberated Russian prisoners had broken into some of the cars looking for something to eat. One car contained barrels of sauerkraut. They were trying to break open the barrels with their bare hands and feet. Another car contained boxes of synthetic jam. Each Russian had a box of jam and was eating it. Some of them literally ate themselves to death.

At the house in which I stayed was a radio that had been rigged so that you couldn't pick up the BBC. I threatened to kick in the side of the radio if they did not get the BBC news, but they said Hitler had fixed it so that they could not hear British broadcasts. They also tried to tell me that they despised Hitler. This I didn't buy. After the way I had been treated, and the things I had witnessed, I could not possibly have believed that they were telling the truth.

We had been told by the American officer that if anyone came near the house we were to shoot to kill, as they were running the show and would not tolerate this kind of conduct.

On the fifth morning, we were walking back toward the town of Ditfurt, five of us, all in step, rifles at the sling. As we approached a row of houses, an American soldier stepped out of a hedgerow onto the road with a Tommy gun. When we got close enough, he raised the Tommy gun and asked, "Who the hell are you guys?"

"Don't you know?" I replied.

He told us, "We only moved in here at four o'clock this morning."

I explained that we were liberated prisoners of war and told him what nationalities we all were. When we had identified ourselves, American soldiers seemed to appear from everywhere. They had their tanks backed into the houses on the street with just the guns pointing out. We were then showered with cigarettes, chocolate bars, and handshakes. These Americans had moved in and had never been told that there were liberated POWs in the town.

The American officer in charge informed us that he would get transportation as soon as it was available to take us back to a captured airfield at Hildersheim where we would be flown out of Germany.

On the sixth day, transportation arrived, but only enough trucks to take out American POWs. The American officer said, "I am not taking out Yanks and leaving the British."

He said, "Get aboard the trucks boys! I'll be back tomorrow to get the remainder."

I was left behind and had to wait another day. With men riding on hoods and fenders, the convoy moved off.

The next day, the trucks returned to take the remainder of us to the airfield. On the way we had to pass through Halberstat. Days earlier, we had witnessed the daylight bombing of Halberstat by at least eight hundred U.S. bombers. The smoke was such that it blocked out the sun. The only things standing were chimneys. Steel beams had melted and were hanging like icicles. The Americans had bulldozed a passageway through the rubble, just wide enough for the tanks and trucks to get through.

At Hildersheim the beautiful American Red Cross women we were almost afraid to talk to supplied us with comfort kits, coffee, and donuts. The U.S. army supplied us with blankets and rations. Here we were deloused and had our first shower in months. The black American attendants could not bear to look at our skeleton-like bodies. Some of them almost threw up. We were billeted in what had been the *Luftwaffe* barracks. There were bullet holes all up the stairs and through the doors. The floors were stained with blood.

The Americans were being flown to LaHavre in Dakotas. We were to wait for British or Canadian aircraft to fly us out. The Dakotas had arrived with supplies with the intention of flying French ex-prisoners of war back to France. These men were overloaded with baggage that consisted of suitcases, pots and pans, and cages with small animals. One man was carrying a crate of chicken. They were told that they were unable to take any possessions aboard the aircraft, which were already overloaded, carrying about thirty to thirty-five men. As they refused to leave this baggage behind, it was decided that they would have to walk back to France. The American officer turned to me and said, "get all the British out here as fast as you can." "We're not going back empty, we will fly you boys to Brussels." Even though this was my first flight, I didn't hesitate for a second as we boarded these beautiful C-47 Dakotas and were flown out of Germany. We landed just outside of Brussels and were met by the RAF, who transported us into the city and handed us over to the British. Here we were checked over by British medical officers, deloused again and issued new uniforms (including underwear) and meal tickets.

Later that evening, we took a train to Ostende, where we boarded a ship for England. My dreams were finally realized. I was heading back to dear old England. On the April 22, 1945, I sent a telegram home from Waterloo railway station to notify my family that I had arrived safely in England. We then proceeded on to Farnborough, where we were admitted into the Fourth Canadian General Hospital. Here I lost contact with the friends I had made on the Death March, as we all went our separate ways. This was the last I saw of Doug and Harry Brailsford.

At the hospital we were deloused yet again and issued new Canadian uniforms. (I still have that uniform all these years later.) We were continually being examined by Canadian medical officers. I remember asking one if he thought I would ever be rid of the lice. He assured me that I would.

I would continually take showers as I still felt dirty. As I had weighed just over eighty pounds when I was liberated, they had me on five meals a day and almost anything else that I asked for.

While at the Fourth General, I had two visitors, both Dieppe men I had known at Stalag VIIIB. They had made a successful escape to neutral Sweden, and from there to the U.K. All they wanted was to return to their units. However, this was not allowed. They were asked to visit other units and tell them of their experiences while in the hands of the Germans. It was a real pleasure for me to meet these two men again. They were both awarded the Military Medal.

I'll never forget the beautiful clean beds, the delicious food, the flowers on the tables, the music, the spotlessly clean nursing sisters, and, most of all, the treatment we received. One evening I was lying on my nice clean bed. A nursing sister came over and asked me why I didn't go out. I said to her, "I never want to leave this place. I have found paradise and if I were to leave, it might not be here when I return."

She answered, "Is it really that good?"

Sixteen
Back in England

Jack was very ill on his arrival back in England. He couldn't keep anything down. He kept throwing up everything, even water, and was wasting away. On V-E Day he knew that he should be in the hospital but pretended he was well. He wanted to witness the celebration as this would fulfill the second wish he had made while a prisoner. It seemed he had survived the Death March and all its horrors by the simple determination to stay alive. On reaching the safety of England, his resistance grew weaker.

While in hospital at Farnborough, I was anxious to make contact with someone I had known before being taken prisoner. I obtained permission from the medical officer to take the train to visit friends nearby in Ashford, Middlesex, who I had not seen since before the Dieppe raid. They were a family I had visited several times before the raid. The lady's name was Mrs. Glanville, and she lived with her daughter and two grandchildren. Mrs. Glanville had another daughter, Mrs. Grant, who lived in my hometown of Kapuskasing, and was a great friend of my mother's. (A third daughter lived in Ealing, near London, and I had visited her several times as well.) It was always a pleasure to visit with the Glanvilles.

As I walked into their house I was met by the mother, daughter, and two granddaughters. They stared at me, as if seeing a ghost. I thought they had forgotten me and asked, "Don't you remember me? It's Jack."

After a few minutes of silence, the daughter said, "We know. But your brother Allan was here yesterday on embarkation leave for the continent." They said he had left to visit their relatives in London before returning to the base. I had not seen my brother for over five years, and was anxious to find him. Unfortunately, he had not told them where he was stationed.

Several hours later, I bade my friends farewell, knowing I would have to try to locate my brother. I travelled to various places where Canadians were or had been stationed, but to no avail. On returning to the hospital I was very ill and running a temperature. They told me I had to stay in bed or they would take my uniform away. However, on the Sunday morning, I explained to the medical officer, a major, that I knew my brother was still in England and that I must find him.

There were two girls at the Fourth Canadian General who had been liberated from a concentration camp in France. Their job was to trace relatives and friends for Canadians who had been prisoners of war. Some of these men had wives in Britain and didn't know where they were. The medical officer told me to get dressed and go and see if one of these girls could locate my brother, and then, if I felt like going back to bed later, to do so.

These girls had the authority to call any of the Canadian military phone numbers. I sat down and picked up the *Star Weekly* while one of the girls called Canadian Military Headquarters London, giving them Allan's name, rank, and regimental number. C.M.H.Q. gave her another number to call. My brother Allan, being the orderly sergeant that day, answered the phone. She passed me the phone and said, "Here's your brother."

Hearing his voice again after all that time was such a shock that I couldn't speak. I couldn't believe how simple it was to find him. He said he would request a pass and get to the hospital as soon as possible. That afternoon, I recognized his walk as he came up a long laneway to the hospital. He walked right past me at the hospital entrance, not recognizing me, and I had to follow him in to the front desk.

After a day or two, the two of us left for London and spent the night before V-E Day there. They gave me a pass and a note stating that I was a liberated POW and if I felt ill at any time, I should go to the nearest hospital.

We witnessed the celebrations, which really were something to behold. I was still having a hard time believing the war was really over. We left the next day by train for Birmingham to visit relatives. We arrived at my uncle's. I sat down at the kitchen table, where I had sat many times before. My aunt was not at home, as she was in the hospital and was very ill. I was so ill, and there was so much excitement about V-E Day and the end of the war, that I hardly noticed that we had been at my uncle's for some time and Uncle Bill still had not spoken to me. It wasn't until he turned to my brother Allan and asked who the friend was that he had brought with him that I realized he couldn't recognize me in the state I was in, even though he had seen me many times before.

At Birmingham, the people would bring me things that I might be able to eat or drink such as milk, cocoa, tea, soup, and arrowroot. I badly wanted to join the celebration but was simply too ill. Towards evening I asked my brother Allan to take me to the nearest hospital, the Queen Elizabeth.

Because of my poor condition and the fact that I was the first liberated POW they had seen, they did not know what to do for me to help me keep my food down.

It was rumoured that nineteen liberated POWs had died while in hospital in Britain. I was told by the house surgeon that it would be at least six months before I would be well enough to return to Canada.

This hospital had a military wing for wounded British servicemen. They had put me in a small single room, thinking that the noise in the big public ward would disturb me. My brother Allan bade me farewell as he had to report back to his unit. This was another shock, having my brother leave me after only a few days. Later, I begged them to take me out of the single room and put me in the big ward with the other men as I could not bear being alone. Girls from British factories in the area would come to visit, bringing cigarettes and goodies. It was a pity being so ill that I could not join in. A girl named Frances would sit at my bedside. However, I did have aunts, uncles, and friends visit me while at the Queen Elizabeth. After my sudden move to Marsden Green, which was out of the city, I had very few visitors.

They kept me alive with injections of liver. As there was very little flesh left on my arms and legs, it was almost impossible to put a needle in. I could not bear to look at my own body. This went on for more than two weeks, and they realized that I was not improving. After my ears and throat became infected, they contacted the Nineteenth Canadian General Hospital, a few miles away at Marsden Green. On visiting the Queen Elizabeth later, the head nurse, who had been very good to me, told me that when they sent me to the Nineteenth General, they did not believe I would survive.

I arrived there on a stretcher, very ill. They would provide me with anything I wanted. I recall the ear, nose, and throat specialist telling a nurse to put me on Frost pain killers and penicillin every four hours. She told me penicillin was a wonder drug, discovered during the war, and only the military hospitals could get it.

For days I was in a state of delirium. The nurses would get other patients to help hold me down. The nights were even worse. There were heavy dark green blackout curtains at the head of my bed. One night I was so delirious that I attempted to climb up these curtains and almost pulled them down. The nurse would wake up the man in the next bed to help control me. After about three weeks, owing to the good food, medication, and excellent treatment, my health was starting to improve.

As my trench mouth kept breaking out while I was a prisoner, I honestly believe that the penicillin finally cleared it up. As I was the only liberated POW in this hospital, I was asked if I minded if the staff and some of the patients came to see me. I said it was perfectly all right.

One day, several blind soldiers and an airman arrived at the hospital. These men had come from St. Dunstan's Home for the Blind. Some of them had wives with them. The hospital was to be a stopover on their way back to Canada. One certainly could not feel sorry for himself upon seeing these men. I had great admiration for them. We used to mix up their tunics as a prank, but they would always be able to pick their own. One evening a nursing sister came to me and asked, "Would you do me a favour and escort these blind boys down to the pub and make sure they get back safely?" I agreed to do so, and this was my first time outside since being transferred to the hospital.

I escorted the men several times.

After about six or seven weeks I was well enough to be discharged. I walked out of the Nineteenth General at Marsden Green a new man. I had my strength back, I felt healthy, and I had put on some weight. Back when I was admitted, the matron stood at the foot of my bed and said, her voice breaking, "What have they done to you boy? I promise that I will put you back on your feet." This they had done.

I went back to the Queen Elizabeth Hospital to visit with and thank them. I looked so different, the nurses could not believe that I was the Canadian who had been in there weeks earlier. They all came rushing up the halls yelling, "Look at the Canadian! Look at what the Canadian Hospital has done for him!"

The matron was so elated, she asked if I would have tea with her. While we were having tea, she asked me if I would do her a favour. I said, "Name it."

She told me that the hospital was full of people who had given up hope, victims of the buzzbombs and the V2 rockets. She wanted me to tour the hospital with her so that she could tell these people what I was like when I came in and what I was like now to assure them that they could recover. When I finally left her that day, there were tears in her eyes.

My aunt was in another hospital, and like some of these people had given up hope. At the Nineteenth General, the staff had found me some oranges. I gave several of these oranges to my uncle to take to my aunt. After my release some weeks later, I found the oranges sitting on the kitchen table in my aunt's home. She had refused them, saying they were meant for me. Several times when visiting at my aunt's home, I would take certain food items that my mother had sent to me to give to my aunt. The next time I would visit, these same items would be put back on the table. When I questioned why she hadn't used them, the answer would be that my mother had sent them for me.

The war years had taken their toll on my aunt, and she passed away shortly after my return to Canada.

I left Birmingham by train for Crookham Crossroads where there was a Canadian army camp. While there, several of us were chosen to go to London and be guests of the King and Queen at a garden party at Buckingham Palace. We marched through the palace to the tune of the "Maple Leaf Forever" played by a military band. The Australians marched through to "Waltzing Matilda." The Queen thanked everyone personally for coming to the aid of Britain. Most of the time there were tears in her eyes. It was great to see King George VI talking and laughing with many of the ex-prisoners of war. We were served cake and ice cream and spent several pleasant hours with Their Majesties.

My brother, Allan, joined me in London and we sat up all night at the Westminster YMCA drinking tea. We were waiting to see the Canadian Armed Forces victory parade through London the next day. The British ATS girl was serving the tea had a cousin, Frances Ward, in our hometown of Kapuskasing who Allan and I knew from our school days.

I was also sent to C.M.H.Q. in London where I was questioned by a cocky young Canadian captain regarding any assistance we might have encountered during the escape attempt. When I mentioned the three airmen, he made an uncomplimentary remark about airmen being out on work parties, even though they had changed over with other prisoners. I took exception to this remark and after looking him up and down, I decided that he was not good enough to shine the airmen's shoes. I wondered how he might have fared had he been in a POW camp instead of at Canada House, where he enjoyed a soft job in the relative safety of England.

When it was apparent that many of us were not returning from the raid, our personal belongings were all put in a sandbag, tagged, and stored. Mine were returned to me while at Crookham Crossroads. The bag contained both my duffel bags and several personal items. Irene's hat badge was not among them. Apparently someone had taken a fancy to it. Prior to being shipped home, we were suddenly moved to Superior repatriation camp. From there we took the train to Southhampton, where we boarded the S.S. *Louis Pasteur* for our return to Canada.

Seventeen
Homeward Bound

In the middle of July 1945, Jack and the other returning troops boarded the S.S. Louis Pasteur, destined for Canada. As they boarded the ship, they once again encountered representatives of the British Red Cross, who were handing out comfort kits. Jack was no stranger to comfort kits, having received kits from the Americans in Germany, the British in Brussels, and the Canadians at Farnborough. The kits contained a toothbrush, toothpaste, a razor, shaving soap, a towel, a facecloth, soap, a comb, and a hairbrush.

During the trip back to Canada, Jack was in the ship's sick bay with pleurisy. On their arrival at Halifax, after consultation, it was decided he was well enough to make the trip to Toronto.

I had to go below deck as the ship pulled away, as I could not bear to see England's shores fade away a second time. I, like many others, had grown to love England.

Shortly after embarking, while lined up for cigarettes, someone tapped me on the shoulder. As I turned around, the man addressed me as Jack. It was Captain Roy Kenny from the Royal Hamilton Light Infantry. He was from my hometown of Kapuskasing, and was getting home early, having volunteered for the Japanese conflict. I couldn't believe he recognized me after all this time. He told me that I didn't have to stand in line and that he would pay for my cigarettes.

Both the *Queen Mary* and *Queen Elizabeth* were in the

harbour as we left, and I was able to see them for the first time. I was amazed at the size of them, but never had the opportunity to get aboard. As I had come down with pleurisy, I spent most of the crossing in the ship's hospital. In a way I was lucky, for many of the other men on board ship had caught scabies from the blankets. During the crossing we were being subjected to inspections for VD, lice, crabs, scabies, and other diseases that we might unintentionally bring back to Canada.

After a six-day voyage, we reached Canada's shores, landing at Halifax Harbour. It all seemed so strange, seeing Canada again after being away for over five years. It would take us quite a while to get used to our own customs again. After disembarking from the *Louis Pasteur*, we boarded trains for Toronto. The coaches were all Pullman cars with sleepers, quite different from the trains we had taken on our last trip to England, which had only wooden seats.

Everything that was happening to us now was positive. We were going home. People were meeting the train at stations. Bands were playing and people were cheering us. The excellent treatment we received from everyone was such a contrast to what I had been used to.

On our arrival in Toronto, the train pulled into the CNE grounds and everyone went through into the stadium, where they would be meeting their relatives. We were all lined up in alphabetical order to receive coupons and money to help us fit back into civilian life. I received $50, food and gas coupons, a train ticket to Kapuskasing, and a pass for a thirty-day leave. As the returning soldiers began to appear in the stadium, the people waiting to meet loved ones cried with joy. I was surrounded by the screams of happiness as family members spotted husbands, sons, and brothers. People were flying down out of the seats, leaping into the arms of loved ones. Amidst all the excitement, I looked up and saw my cousin Bill Floyd and his mother, my Aunt Floss, who were there to meet me, as my father's train from Kapuskasing was late. It was a great feeling that someone I knew was there to welcome me back to Toronto. Aunt Floss had travelled to Kapuskasing to help comfort her sister (my mother) when I was reported "missing in action." A few months later, Bill was reported "missing" over Germany while with the RCAF. Bill's aircraft, a Lancaster, had been shot down over the Zuider Zee while returning from a bombing mission. After being picked up by the Germans, he finished up as a POW in Stalag Luft III, which was made famous by the Great Escape.

Shortly after arriving at my aunt's home, my father arrived. We embraced at the door, the only time we had ever done this. At first it was hard to start a conversation as I did not know where to begin, for there were so many things to catch up on. After lunch, my father and I left for the Parliament Buildings as I had to renew my driver's licence, which had been confiscated by the Germans. As my dad knew many people there, including several ministers, I received a very warm welcome, as people came pouring out of offices wanting to meet me and welcome me back. On leaving, we made our way to Bloor Street and boarded a street car. My father had to go to the Ford plant to have his dealer's franchise confirmed. We entered the car and sat down. Sitting across from us was Jeanette Mitchell, who we both knew from Kapuskasing. She recognized my father right away. She had lost her husband, George, who was serving in the navy on a minesweeper. We were well received at the Ford plant, and when it became known that I had arrived back from overseas that day, I was being deluged with questions and good wishes.

That evening we boarded the train for Kapuskasing at St. Clair Avenue station. It was a relief to be alone at last with my father, where we could reminisce about years gone by, which rekindled memories that had helped me survive and keep my sanity. I had a million questions to ask. We sat up all night in the smoking room, and talked about farming again. He told me there were over eighty acres of hay that needed cutting. The farm had been a thriving dairy business, supplying much of Kapuskasing with milk, and had been carved out of one hundred acres of bush by him. He had been given the land when he returned from the Great War. He had returned in 1916 after being wounded in France. When he recovered from his wounds he was sent to Kapuskasing, where he had been given land under the Returned Soldiers and Sailors Settlement Scheme. There he developed what became known as Poplar Farm Dairy, which included a herd of purebred Holstein cows, milked by machine.

It is hard to explain the feelings I was having at the time, as every mile was bringing me closer to home. I would soon be able to see the farm I had been raised on. Seeing it would bring back memories of my departure more than five years earlier, when I watched the farm fade away in the distance, leaving an ache in my heart.

Eventually, the train stopped at Monteith, where there was a German prisoner of war camp. This aroused my curiosity, as we had been instructed that all German prisoner of war camps were out of bounds. My father, as a member of the Veterans' Guard, had been stationed there. Apparently the Canadian government did not want us to see how well the Germans had been treated.

During these last hours on the train, I was preparing myself for my initial reunion with my mother and the rest of my family. I was very anxious as I did not know what I would say or how I would greet them. Would I smile or cry? I went to the washroom and when I returned to the coach where my dad and I had been sitting, there before my eyes were my mother, sister, and brother. They had boarded the train at Moonbeam, the last stop before Kapuskasing. I stood in shock, unable to speak. It was like a dream. I had mixed emotions: I was happy to see my mother and sister and brother, but I had planned to meet them at Kapuskasing and I had rehearsed and rehearsed my first words to them. It hurt me deeply that I could not say what I was feeling.

Finally, the train pulled into Kapuskasing. I was greeted by almost two hundred people who were there to meet me. On the farm, they had decorated the whole house, including the kitchen, and there was a huge "Welcome home, Jack" sign outside. It was a great feeling to be back home again. It brought tears to my eyes and left me speechless. And there was Mum's good cooking to look forward to.

My first night home was disappointing. I wanted to be alone with my family to thank my mother for the parcels she had sent me while I was a POW and for always believing that one day I would return home safely. Mum had gone to a lot of trouble getting the parcels away and finding the things to put in them, which always seemed to be the things that I needed most. Somehow she seemed to know just what I was most in need of. My younger brother Victor gave up sugar so that it could be sent to me. I just wanted to sit and talk and maybe shed a tear or two. However, a pair of uninvited guests arrived. They were friends of the family and had even been married in our home many years earlier. This changed all my plans as I was being plied with questions that I was not in the proper frame of mind to answer. The man offered to sell me a Model A Ford for $400 (my father had sold it to him a year before for $200). It was a great relief to me when they decided to leave, as their visit had come at a time when I was not thinking too clearly. I wanted to remember all the times I had sat at the dining room table for Christmas dinners and the parties that we had had in the house — including three weddings. I tried to picture in my mind what the Christmas trees had looked liked.

The second night home, my father, who never attended the movies, wanted to see a film called *Drums*. I was asked if I would like to go, and I agreed, not knowing what I was in for. For the entire film, I sat and watched scenes of a Scottish Regiment being ambushed and wiped out by tribesmen in India. It was hard for me to deal with after all the horror I had seen and experienced. It just added to my trauma.

Within days of returning, I retraced each step I had walked as a young boy and visited all the favourite spots that my brother and I had considered almost sacred. I thought of how, as a child, I was always fascinated by any type of machinery. I would look forward in anticipation to thrashing time, running home from school to watch the thrashing machine and marvelling at how the engine worked. How I loved the smell of the engine that in 1931 almost killed my father. I stood where years earlier my younger brother Ken had drowned in the creek that ran through the farm. I wondered if, had he lived, he would have been in the service like his two older brothers. I remembered as an eight-year-old how this tragedy had affected my parents. I remembered listening to conversations I was not supposed to hear about how the farm would have to be sold because they could not live here anymore and would have to move away. I hoped and prayed — which was all I could do as an eight-year-old — that this would not happen.

The barn and other buildings had been empty since before the war, owing to the Depression, and were in a run-down condition. Most of the implements were missing. It was as though the farm had been picked clean, while my dad, my brother, and I were serving our country. To see the farm in this state was very depressing. I realized that starting the farm up again would be a tremendous undertaking, especially since there were no materials available (such as lumber, nails, and cement) as the War Time Prices and Trades Board was still in effect. It would be months or years before any of these items would be available.

I had to have a permit signed by the chief of police to prove that I needed a bicycle to travel to work, and waited several months to get it. This was an awful insult, after serving my country for over five years.

It took the family dog some time getting used to me in uniform. Several times he went for me when I was coming home after dark. When I started working and was wearing overalls, he went for me a few times when coming home from work. I guess I should have seen this coming: he also had a go at me over five years earlier at my brother Tom's when I was home on my last leave.

One day I was visited by a young lad from Hearst, Ontario, whose brother was reported missing after the Dieppe raid and never found. He told me his mother still had hopes that he might be wandering around France with amnesia. She wanted my opinion as to whether there was a slim chance that he was still alive. It was very difficult for me, as I could see that there was hope in his eyes that his brother might still be alive. I tried to explain that thousands of Allied troops had overrun France, and if he were alive he would surely have turned up. There was little chance that he was still alive.

Jack, back at home, in 1945.

During my thirty days leave, I was having trouble sleeping and was having nightmares. It was apparent that something was bothering me. I would continually wake up in a cold sweat, raving, and would scare my young brother Victor, who slept in the same room. It was evident that I had a serious problem. This condition lasted for years.

I began to notice that whenever I would try and start up a conversation, someone would change the subject. This would really bother me, and many things would go through my mind as I was wondering why they were doing this. As it turned out, unbeknown to me, the Red Cross had advised my parents that they should encourage me not to talk about my experiences.

It was awfully hard getting used to Canadian customs again. I was missing England, and I was thinking seriously about going back.

Later, I was to suffer from severe depression and considered suicide. Many things were bothering me, and as depression was unheard of at that time, no one could see that I had a problem. These bouts of depression would hit me without warning. How could I cope with it? I had to contend with it alone.

One problem I had was the guilt that I was alive and others were not. Another was that the other boys who were coming home were victorious soldiers, whereas I was a liberated POW. This bothered me considerably. I was also haunted by memories of the after-effects of the chain-up and, of course, the Death March. Since leaving home I had witnessed many things: horror, grief, bravery, and death. I had seen the worst and the best of mankind.

It was very difficult for anyone having been a POW to fit back into civilian life. The only people that I wanted to be with were the returning servicemen, as we had something in common.

I had suffered tremendous stress and there was nowhere to get help. While a prisoner in Germany, I had made promises to myself that I realized I would not be able to keep. I had to find something to do that would not be boring to me. I would have to have my mind at ease and enjoy whatever I chose to do. So as you see, I was fighting an awful battle within myself. Regardless, I was grateful to be back among family and friends, home again on the farm where I had spent so many happy years. My dream had been fulfilled.

While I was on leave, the war in the Pacific came to an end. I will always remember the celebrations. The engineer on the train blew his whistle all the way from Cochrane to Kapuskasing. There were car horns blowing and people dancing in the street. It was like V-E Day all over again. With my leave coming to an end, I had to return to Toronto, back to the CNE grounds once more, to be discharged from the Canadian army. This again was a shock to me, as in the army, all of our needs were looked after. Now I would be entirely on my own. I felt as though I was lost. I left the CNE grounds with my discharge paper that day, September 10, 1945. This would bring an end to my service with the Canadian army, leaving me with no regrets and feeling proud that I had played a small part in a tremendous fighting machine: the Canadian army. I knew I had served my country honourably. Now I would have to hang up my uniform, get a job, and work for a living.

I was hired by the town as a carpenter; being raised on a farm, one learns many things. The first job I was given was to make a set of steps. After being in the service for over five years, this was a quite a task. I had never made a set of steps before. Then I was laying hardwood floors and asphalt shingles. I had shingled lots of roofs with cedar shingles, but never asphalt shingles. However, I managed until the cold weather set in. Then, they gave me a job in the paper mill, in what was known as the ground-wood department. This was a very boring job, but at least I was inside for the winter. I was offered several better jobs that were all shift work, but having worked shift work in that mill before the war, I knew I would never be able to handle it. Having applied to the millwrights and the pipe fitters and the blacksmith shop — all daytime work — I received the same reply: they could not hire me as I had no experience.

I was starting to feel claustrophobic working inside, and so, for the second time in my life, I left the Spruce Falls employ. Instead, I started driving a gravel truck that had to be loaded by hand. I enjoyed doing this, and shovelling the gravel helped build up my body strength. While driving the truck, people kept telling me that I should get my own truck and work for myself. This happened to be one of the promises that I had made to myself while a prisoner of war in Germany. However, it wasn't that simple. First, I had to have a permit from the War Time Prices and Trades Board. In order to get that, I needed promises in writing, which I asked for and got, proving that I would have work for the truck.

The three-ton Ford was finally ordered in August of that year. Against the advice of several people, who told me I was making a bad mistake, I decided to go ahead. However, trucks were very slow coming off the assembly line, and each dealer had to wait his turn. With the months passing by and the work I had been promised slipping away, I decided to leave for Toronto and apply at the Department of Veterans' Affairs for a six-month mechanics course. This would give me two years on a five year apprenticeship — at least this would get the word "labourer" off my social insurance card. (When I was discharged, I was given a social insurance card with the word "labourer" on it, which I took as an insult. "Labourer" was about as low as you could get.) I was asked if I would consider going to London, Ontario, as there was a class just starting up. I agreed.

The truck I had been waiting for was finally delivered to the dealer in January of the following year, but by that time, I was half way through my course. I decided it was just as well that I did not wait for the truck, for now I was finally starting to get on with my life.

Dieppe Cemetery, forty-five years after the raid.

Epilogue

I am convinced that the Germans *did* know of the Dieppe raid in advance, and those who planned it were aware of this. The Germans' knowledge of the invasion was evident when the *Luftwaffe* attacked the two ships carrying the Royal Regiment on what was to be Operation Rutter, and then again in Littlehampton. As prisoners, the Germans told us they had been waiting for us for ten days.

It was also very unusual that, when we were preparing for Operation Rutter, we were told to have absolutely no identification (except our identification disks). That meant no photos, shoulder flashes, letters, etc. We were to carry nothing that would identify us. With Operation Jubilee, there was no such order.

It should have been obvious when the aerial photographs were taken of the main beach that it would be impossible for the Churchill tanks to navigate on the stones there.

It was apparent that the operation was meant to fail, to convince Stalin and Roosevelt that a second front across the English Channel was not possible in 1942. However, it appeared to us at the time that the Germans were convinced that the raid was an attempted second front.

After my return, I kept in touch with some of the men whose names I have mentioned in the story. For years I corresponded with the two South African brothers, an Australian, and a New Zealander. Jim Mawbey was back working for a paving company in Toronto. Upon Red Perry's arrival in Toronto, he hired a taxi to drive him to every hotel and Legion Hall until he found Jim Mawbey. (Later, Red Perry returned to Timmins and went back to gold mining.) This was an example of the comradeship that existed among us.

Pete Kelly was killed in the raid. Each time I have gone back to Dieppe, I have visited his grave.

I met Garth White, also from Timmins, at a gas station in Kenogami, Ontario. Garth had lost his trigger finger to a German sniper. He'd had the rifle shot right out of his hands. He told me he would be leaving shortly for British Columbia.

George Pelletier apparently disappeared from the face of the earth. The last time I saw him at Stalag VIIIB he was going out on a working party as a change-over to make an escape attempt. No one has seen or heard of him since.

I remember seeing Company Sergeant Major Norm MacIver on the beach with an eye hanging down on his cheek. Apparently a German bullet had entered the side of his head and knocked the eye out of its socket. Some years later in Toronto, he told me that the Germans had put the eye back in and he could see out of it

Over the years I would also learn the fates of the three men who I made my first escape attempt with. The Canadian known as Denny was a Hurricane pilot from the Ottawa area. He had

Escapees meet again after thirty years. Jack Poolton on the left, and Canadian airman Bill Denison on the right.

Jack in front of the Royal Regiment memorial at Puys.

In 1992, fifty years after the Dieppe raid, Jack stands on the beach where the Royals landed.

been shot down by a "Flak" over France in 1942 while coming in low to strafe a machine-gun emplacement. The Flak hit his engine and he crash landed. Thirty years later through the Legion Magazine, I found him. His name was Bill Denison and he lived in Ottawa. We still meet occasionally.

Ian Gilmour was shot down over Africa in a Wellington bomber. He had lived just outside of London, England. The last time I saw him was as I left Stalag VIIIB in January 1945 on what became known as the Death March. Over the years I tried to find him, but to no avail.

The third man, who I believe was named George Thatcher, had been a wireless operator and navigator and was shot down in a Lancaster bomber over Germany.

It was a privilege for me to have known and travelled with these airmen. The way they could read the stars at night continues to fascinate me to this day.

Regimental Sergeant Major Harry Beesley of the Third Commando, who had been our leader and benefactor in the Dieppe Compound at Stalag VIIIB and had stood up to the Germans many times on our behalf, was sent to a POW camp at Blechammer near Kosel Upper Silesia and was not sent to Stalag IID at Stargard with the Canadians. On Christmas Day 1944, he escaped and eventually reached the Russian front. Then, in February 1945, at Krakow, Poland, after being liberated by the Russians, Harry Beesley was killed in a train accident on the way to Odessa.

In 1992, while in Dieppe to attend the fiftieth anniversary of the raid, I met two German *Luftwaffe* pilots who had flown against us on that fateful day. They were talking to three Canadian air force veterans who had fought in the skies against them. As I watched the Canadian airmen shake hands with the Germans, one of the Germans turned to me and extended his hand. For a moment, I hesitated, wondering if I could shake hands with the enemy, even after fifty years. I took his hand and shook it firmly, thinking that if the airmen could shake his hands, so could I.